ABC Reading eggs

# My First Handwriting

By Sara Leman

Ages 4–6

Dear Parent or Carer,

This book is part of the **My First** series of **Reading Eggs** workbooks. **Reading Eggs** has proven to be very popular with parents, children and teachers. The **Reading Eggs** books and website have helped more than 20 million children worldwide learn to read.

Each vibrant book in the **My First** series includes a wide range of interesting activities that will help your child develop essential reading and writing skills. Written by experienced teachers and educators, the series supports what your child learns at school.

The pages are clear and uncluttered, with activities that build real skills. Activities are fun and motivate children to continue working and learning. Instructions are easy to follow and regular challenges entice children to extend their learning.

I hope that you and your child enjoy using this and other books in the series.

Kind regards, Katy Pike
Publisher

**ABC Reading Eggs** My First Handwriting

ISBN: 978-1-74215-173-1


Reprinted 2011, 2013 (twice), 2014, 2015, 2016, 2018, 2019, 2020, 2021, 2022, 2024, 2025

Distributed by:
Pascal Press
PO Box 250
Glebe NSW 2037

www.readingeggs.com
Written by Sara Leman
Publisher: Katy Pike
Editors: Sandra Iannella and Amanda Santamaria
Design and layout by Modern Art Production Group
Printed in China by 1010 Printing International Ltd

# Contents

# Letter Formation Chart

## Warm up fun!

## Straight lines and downstrokes

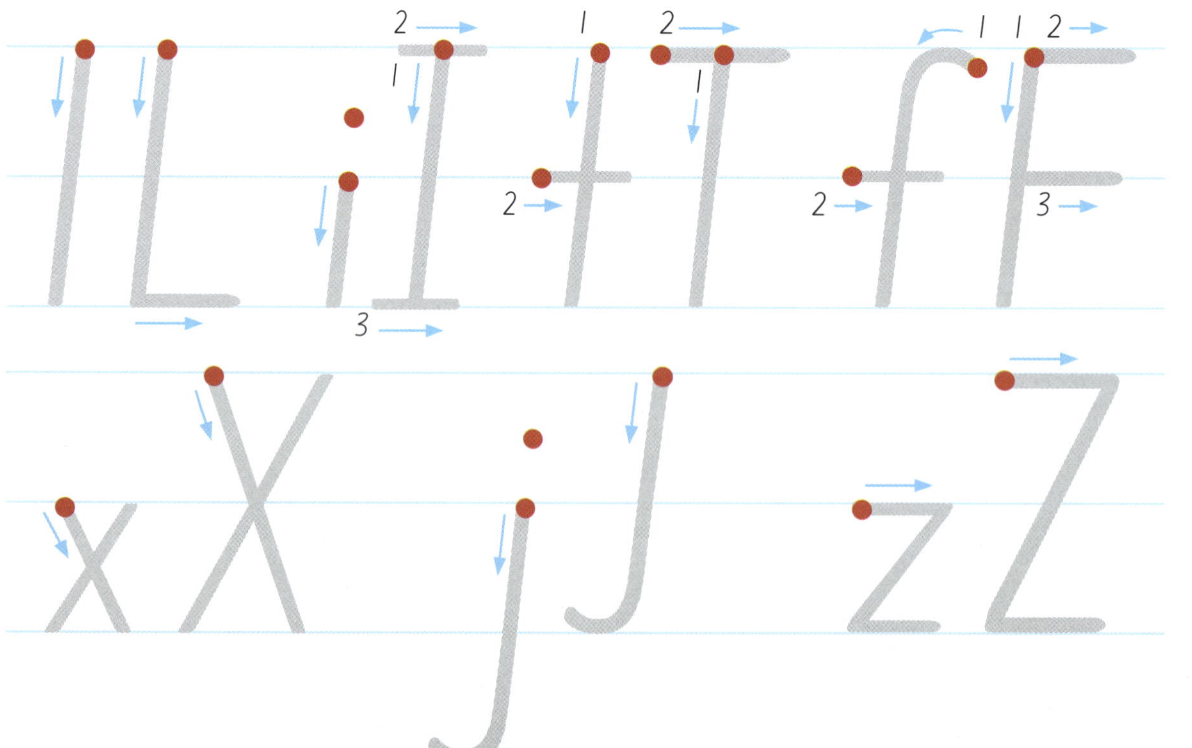

## Anticlockwise waves 1

aA cC oO uU iV uW eE sS

## Anticlockwise waves 2

dD qQ yY gG

## Clockwise letters

nN mM rR hH bB kK pP

# Additional Activities for Parents

Ensure your child is using the correct pencil grip.

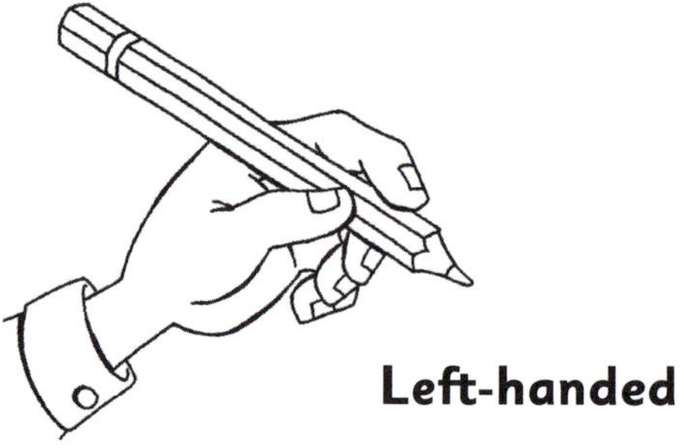
**Left-handed**

**Right-handed**

Ensure that your child's writing book is correctly positioned.

**Left-handed**

**Right-handed**

Keep pencils sharpened for greater accuracy and control.

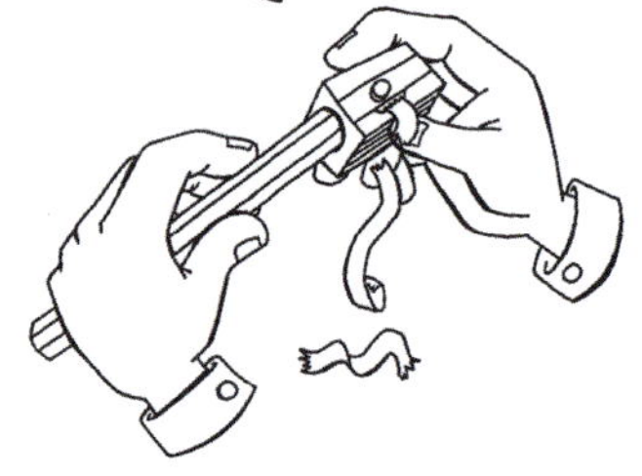

Remind your child to keep both feet flat on the floor. Make sure that they keep their non-writing hand on the table. This hand is used to secure their book or paper.

Tracing over dotted lines is a useful skill for developing fine motor control and teaching letter formation.

Tracking letters is also a useful practice for encouraging letter formation.

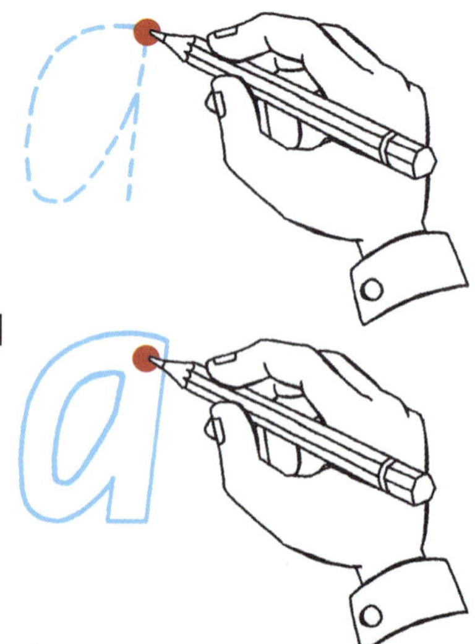

**Pre-writing exercises can be fun for your child and an ideal way to warm up fine-motor muscles.**

Try:

- **The pincer pinch:** Pinch the index finger and thumb together several times before gripping the pencil.
- **The wrist roll:** Roll the wrists six times in a clockwise direction. Repeat in an anti-clockwise direction. Vary the speed from quick to slow.
- **Zig-zags:** Quickly zig-zag the wrists up and down ten times. Repeat but much more slowly.
- **Loops:** Loop the wrists in a clockwise, figure-of-eight direction. Repeat in an anti-clockwise direction
- **The shake:** Vigorously shake the wrists ten times. Repeat.

Fine motor skills can be developed and practised in a variety of ways:

- fastening and unfastening buttons
- modelling with play dough
- threading beads
- pegging
- sewing
- tearing paper
- picking up small objects with tweezers
- using fingers to find buried objects in rice or sand
- drawing and doodling with a variety of pens, pencils and crayons
- transferring coloured water or paint using droppers
- tracing letters and shapes with fingertips
- cutting out shapes with scissors

Encourage your child to trace carefully over dotted lines. Alternatively, they can track mazes.

Provide your child with a writing area or a box filled with supplies. Fill it with a variety of paper, e.g. card, tracing paper, lined paper, sticky notes, envelopes and mini notebooks. It should also contain several implements e.g. pencils, crayons, markers, erasers, sharpeners, scissors and glue. Always encourage your child to experiment with their writing.

Create a writing-on-the-go kit that contains a range of writing implements and stationary. Put everything in a zip-lock bag and take it with you when you go out. Your child will then be able to write anytime, anywhere!

Write notes to your child and encourage them to write back to you. Even if your child is at the emergent literacy stage and is unable to read, writing notes is an excellent activity to promote writing for a purpose and to encourage letter formation.

# Lesson 1 • Warm up fun

1 Follow Jet Set's trails. Start at the dot.

2 Swim through Wheely Whale's waves.

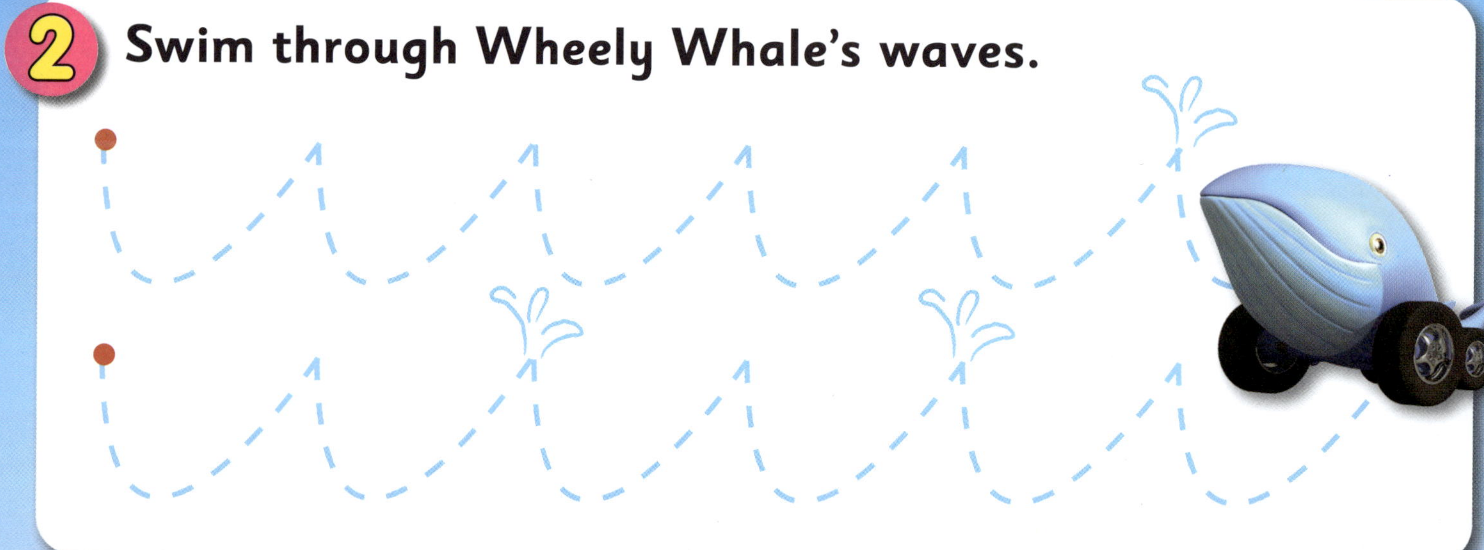

3 Follow Sunny Snails trails.

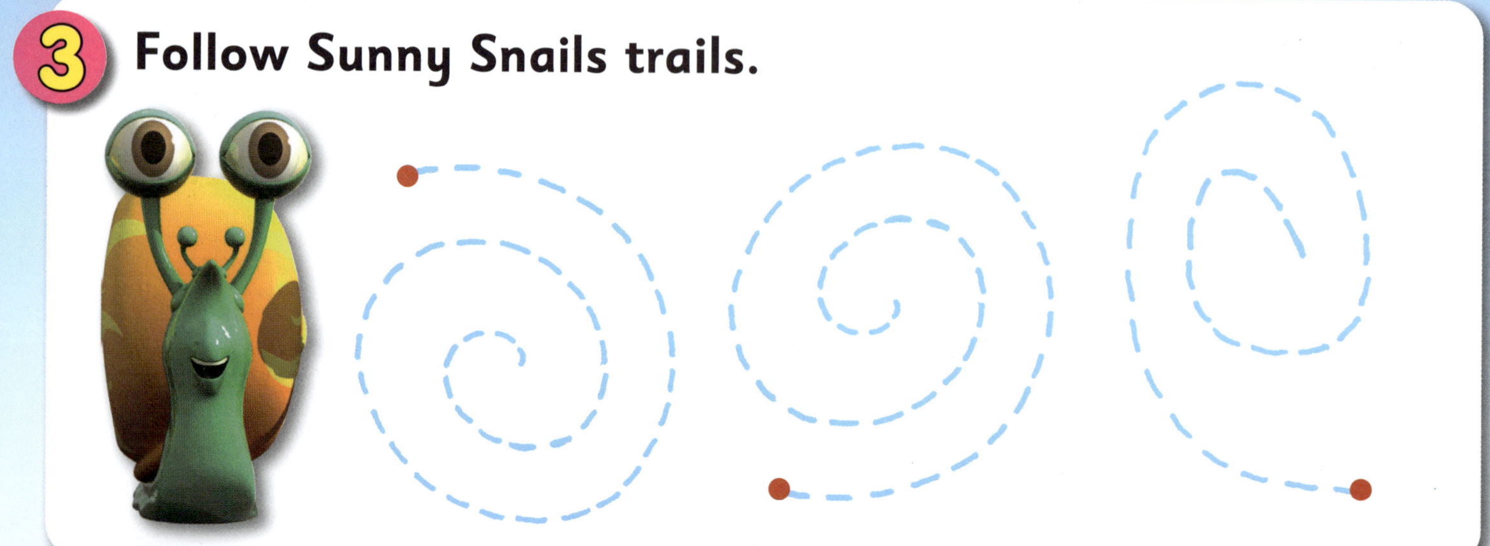

## 4 Slither with Jake Snake.

## 5 Fly with Flutter Bye Bye.

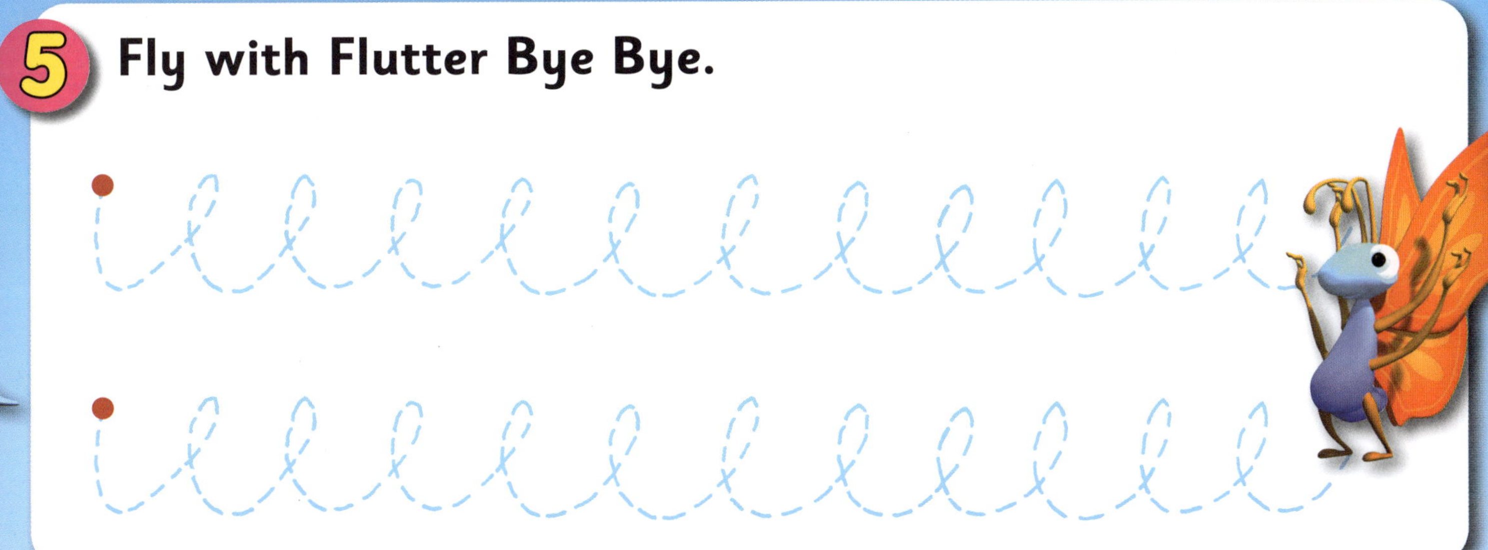

## 6 Hop along with Frogfish.

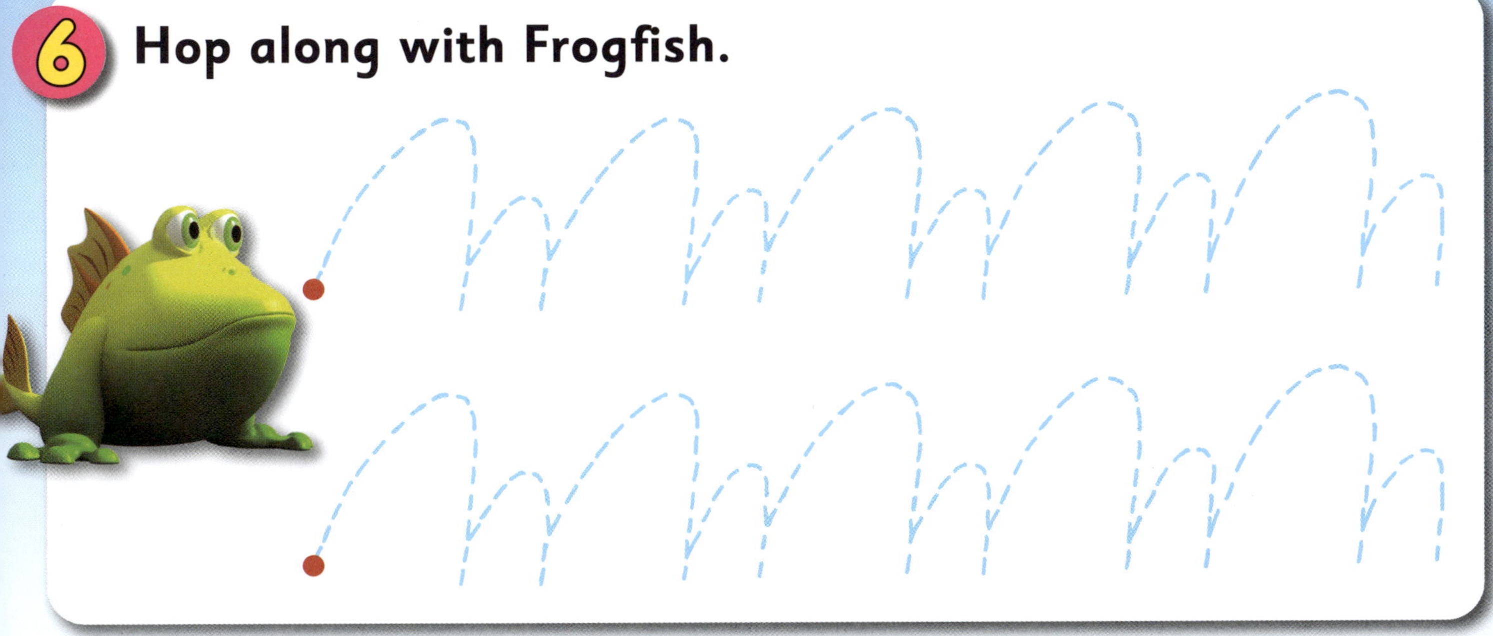

# Il

## Lesson 2

Trace.

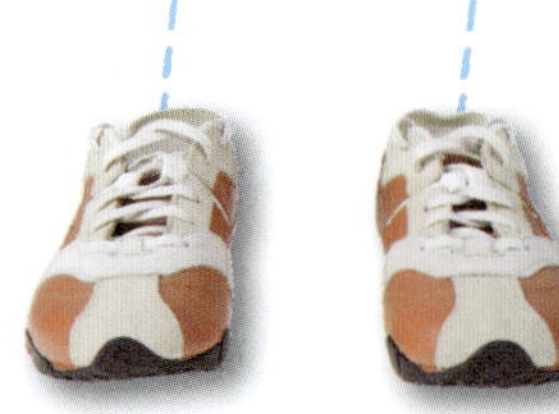

legs

**1** Complete Airy Fairy's wands.

**2** Trace the dotted lines.

## 3 Finish Meg's candles.

## 4 Complete the gifts.

## 5 Trace and write.

# iI
## Lesson 3

Trace.

**1** Complete the flag poles.

**2** Track.

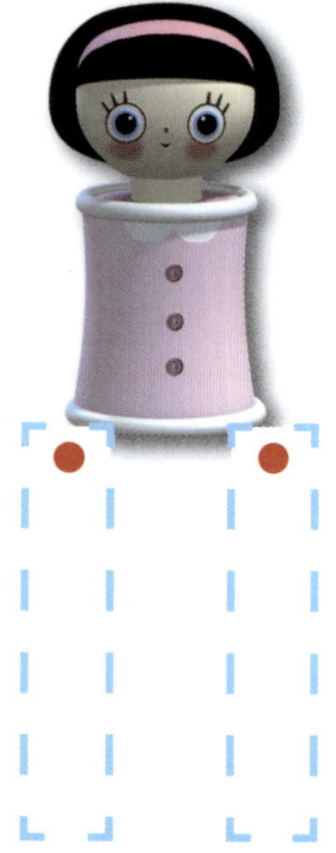

Peggy Leg's legs

A flower for Zee the Bee

## 3 Complete Icy Mice's friends.

## 4 Track.

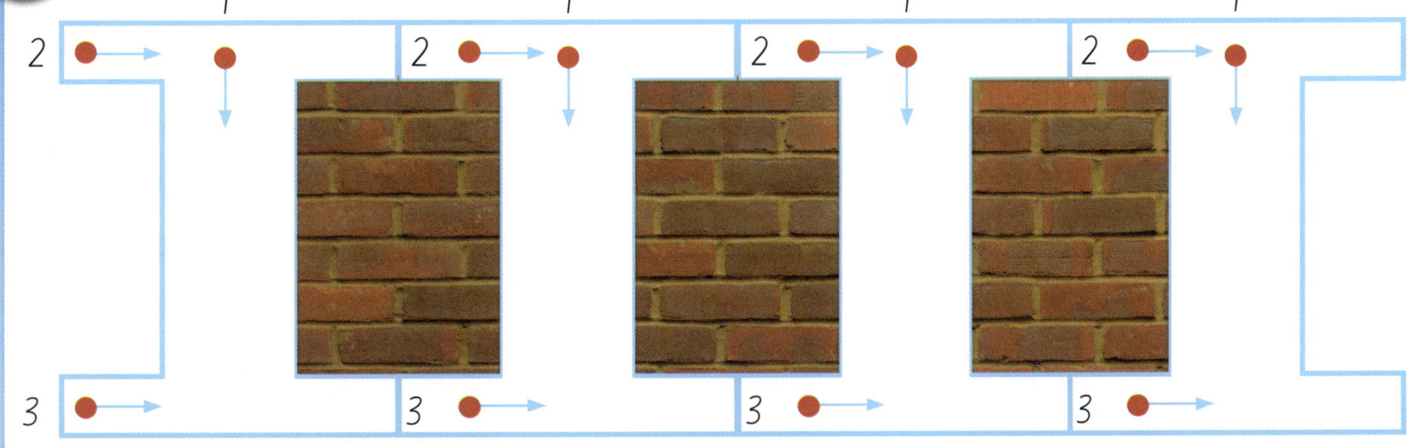


## 5 Trace and write.

# tT Lesson 4

Trace.

tree

1 Finish the fence.

2 Complete the scarecrows. Draw some clothes.

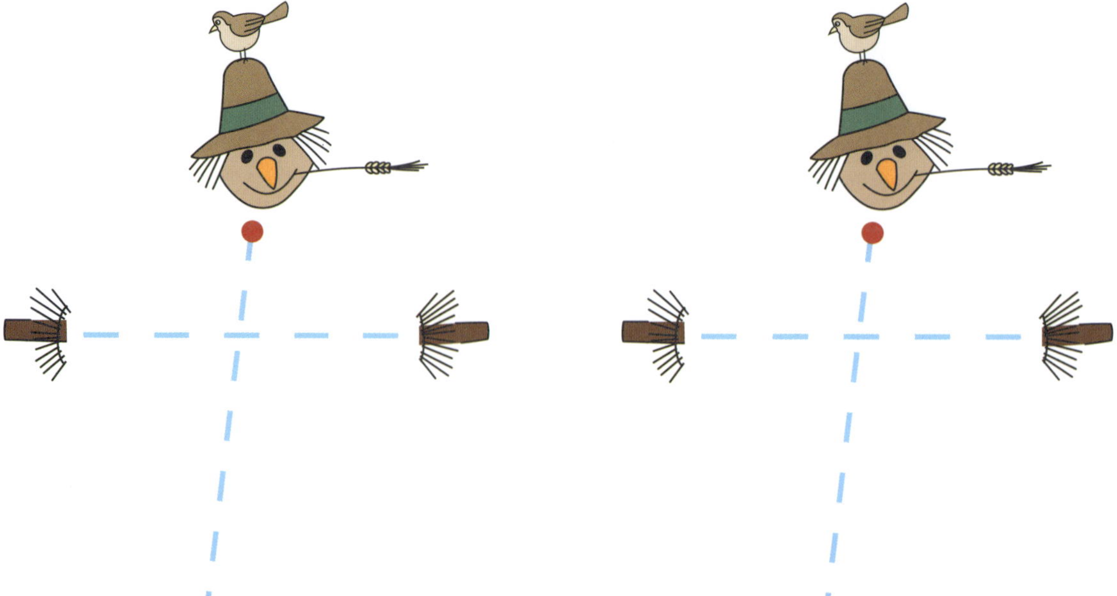

## 3 Trace the dotted lines.

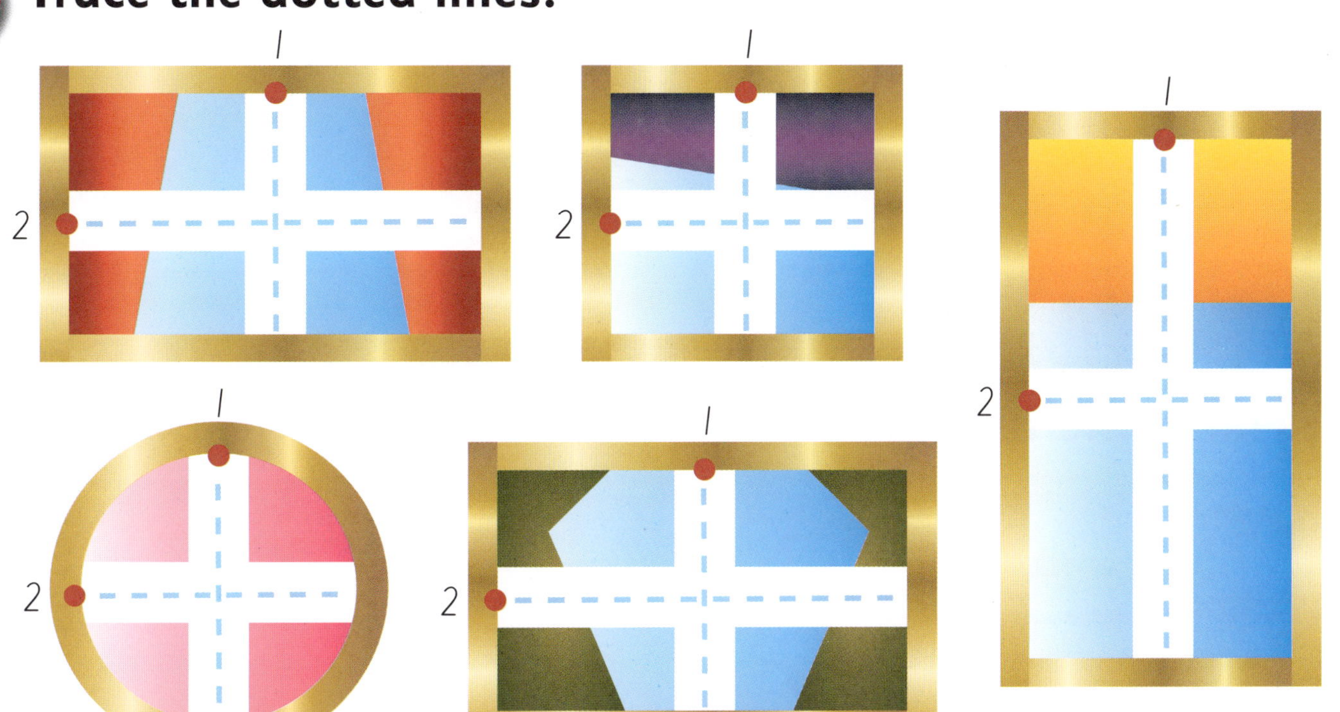


## 4 Trace.

## 5 Trace and write.

Trace.

jar

**1** Finish the fishing hooks. Draw some more jellyfish.

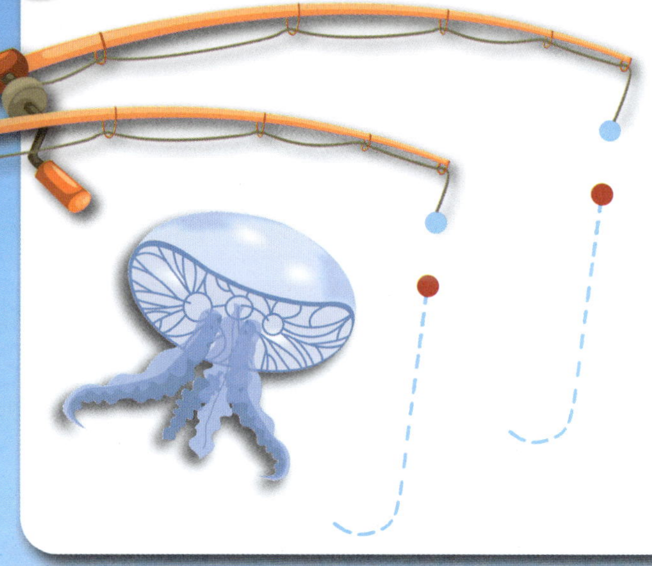

**2** Add some more curls.

## 3 Complete Dotty Sun Spot's umbrellas.

## 4 Trace the dotted lines.

## 5 Trace and write.

# fF Lesson 6

Trace.

flower

1 Complete the caterpillars.

2 Trace the candy canes.

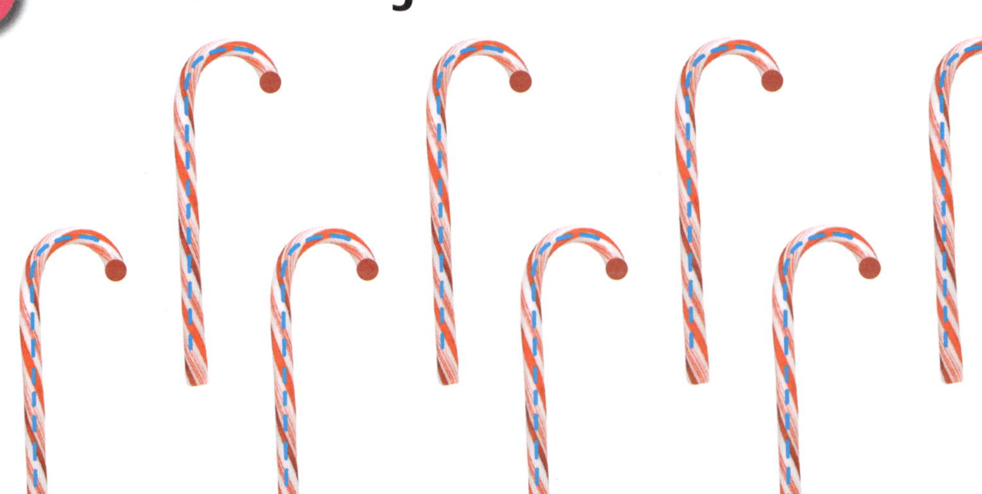

How many candy canes?

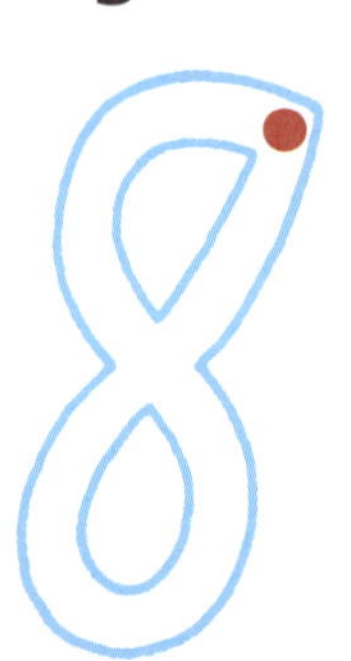

## 3 Finish Flutter Bye Bye's flowers.

## 4 Complete the windows.

## 5 Trace and write.

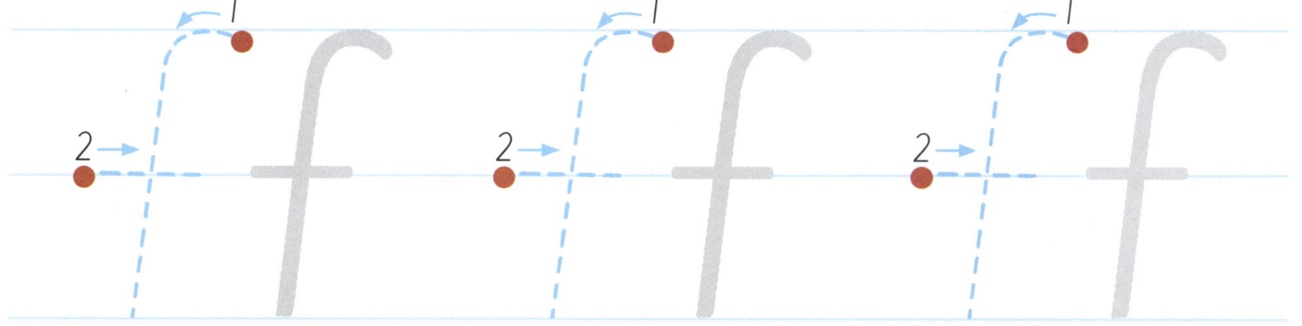

Trace.

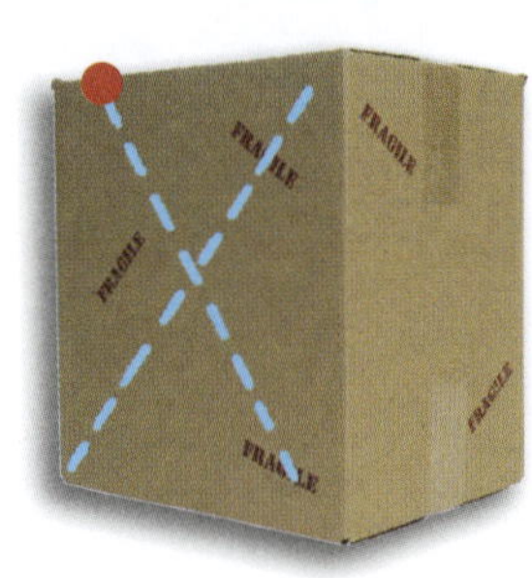

box

1 Help Sixty Six reach the finish line. Follow the track.

2 Trace Shoe Sheep's laces.

## 3 Slice the pizzas.

## 4 Trace the dotted lines on these flags.

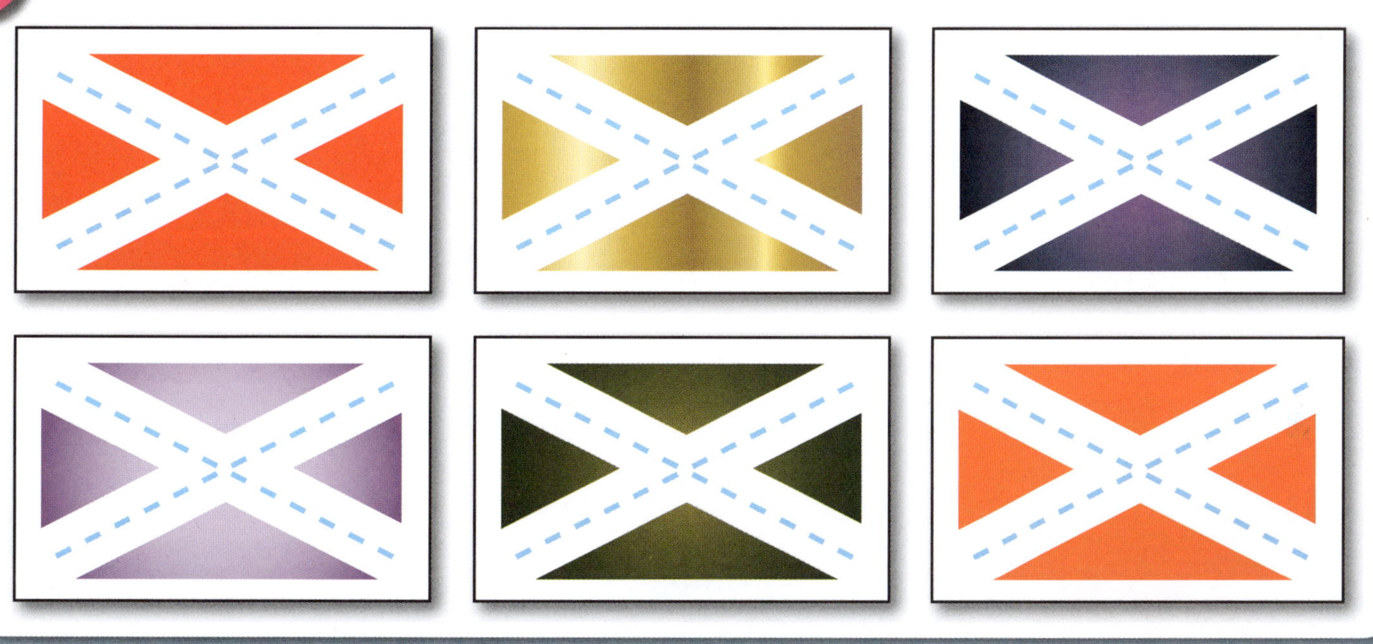

## 5 Trace and write.

x X x X x X x X

# zZ Lesson 8

Trace.

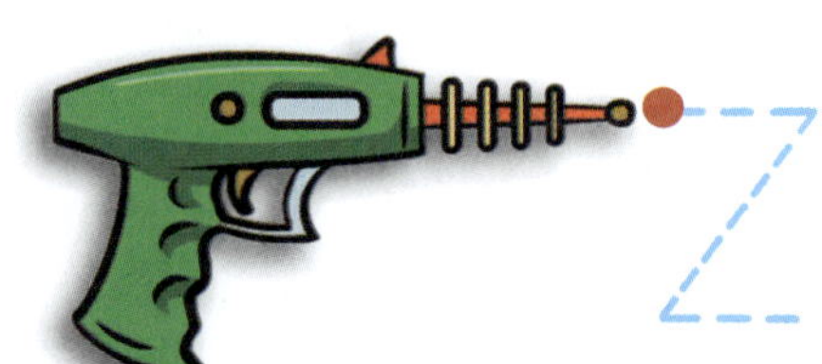

zap

1 Help the critters find their food. Draw their path.

2 Track the lightning bolts.

## 3 Draw.

Go Go Gizmo's legs

Giddy Up's spring

## 4 Trace Happy Nap's snores.

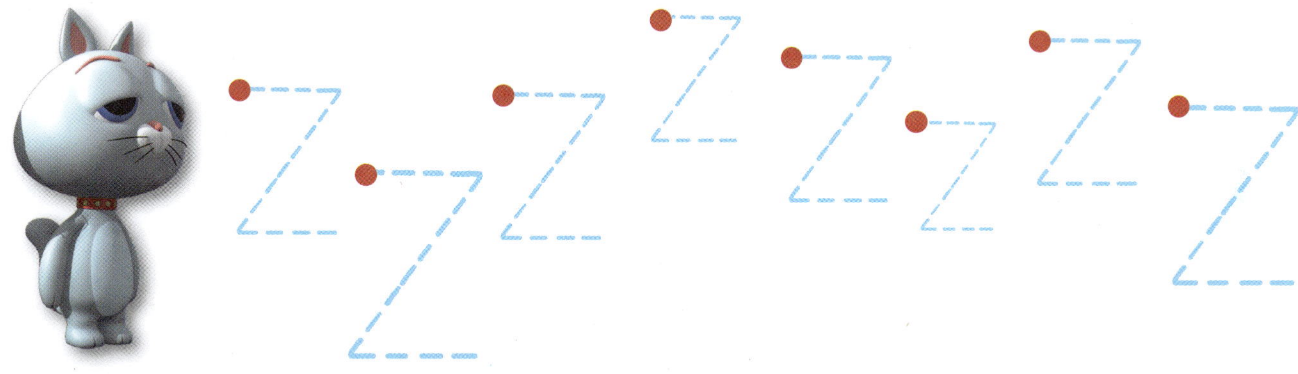

## 5 Trace and write.

z z z z z z z z

# Fun spot 1

**1** **Help Octo Puss get home to her cave.**

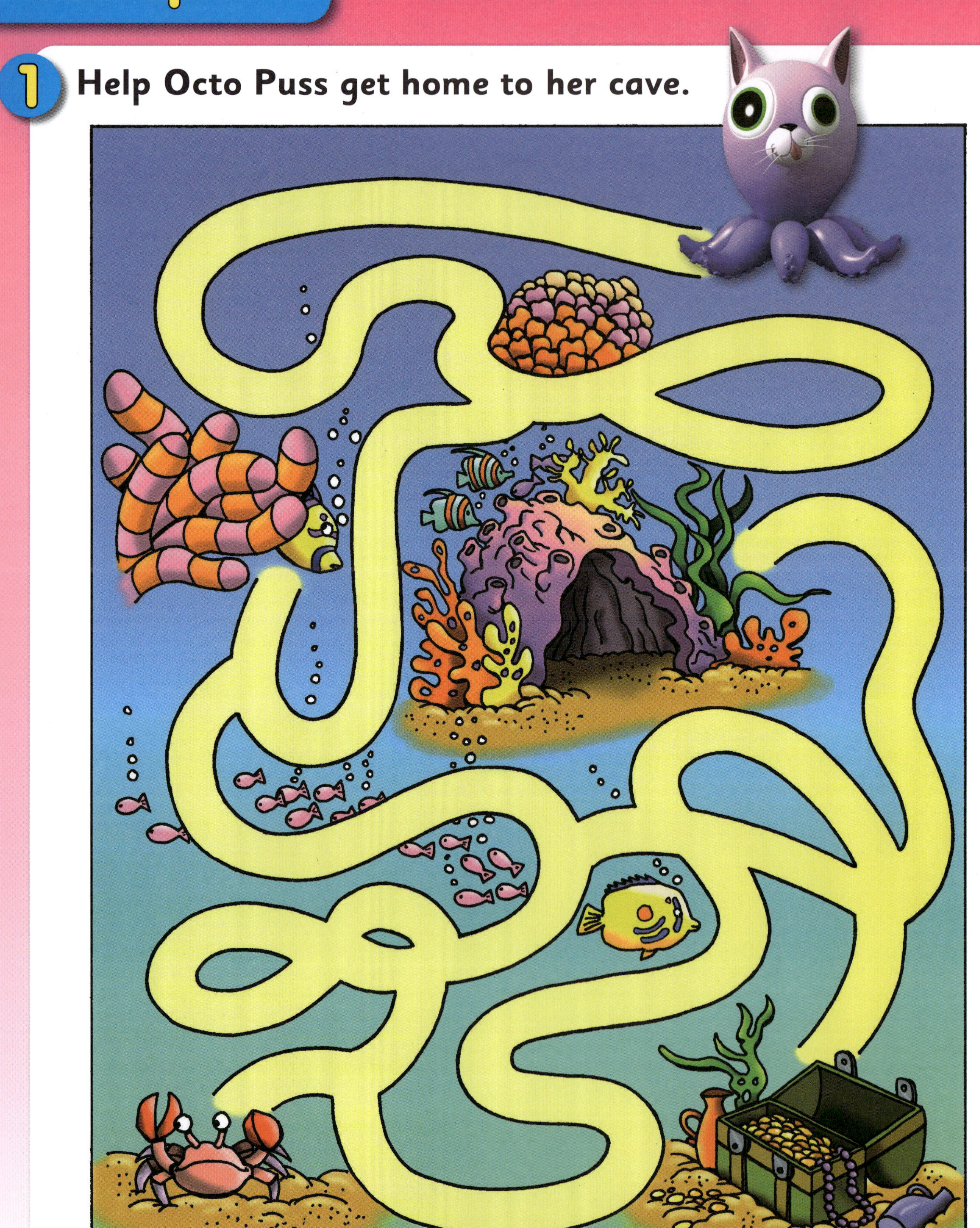

## 2 Complete each critter and then colour.

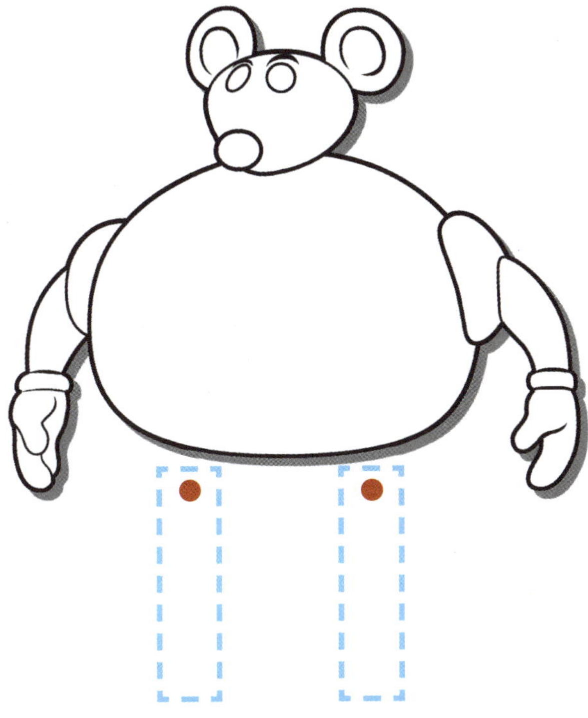

Marshmallow Mouse

Yabby Dabby Doo

Bow Tie Magpie

Thingamabob

# Review 1

**Complete each word. Join to the correct picture.**

lollipop

taxi

Jelly Jag

giraffe

picnic

Tiger Turtle

zig zag

x-ray

Icy Mice

Ladbug

# aA
## Lesson 9

Trace.

**1** Trace Tug Boat Bug's waves.

**2** Help Appley Ant find his apple. Start at the red dot.

**3** Trace the ladybugs.

**4** Climb up and down the mountains.

**5** Trace and write.

# cC
## Lesson 10

Trace.

1 **Draw a tail on Catty Cake.**

2 **Track the patterns on the cake.**

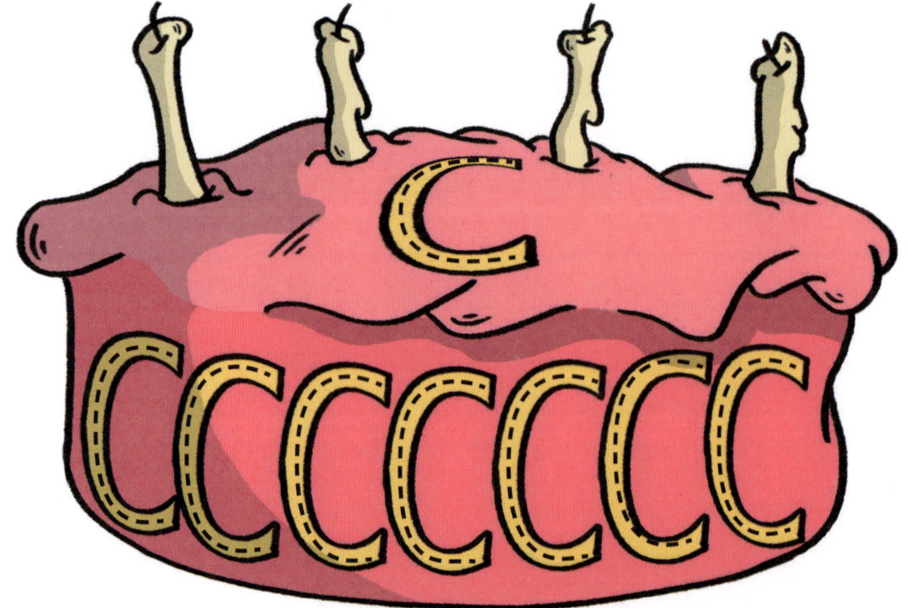

## 3 Complete the cats.

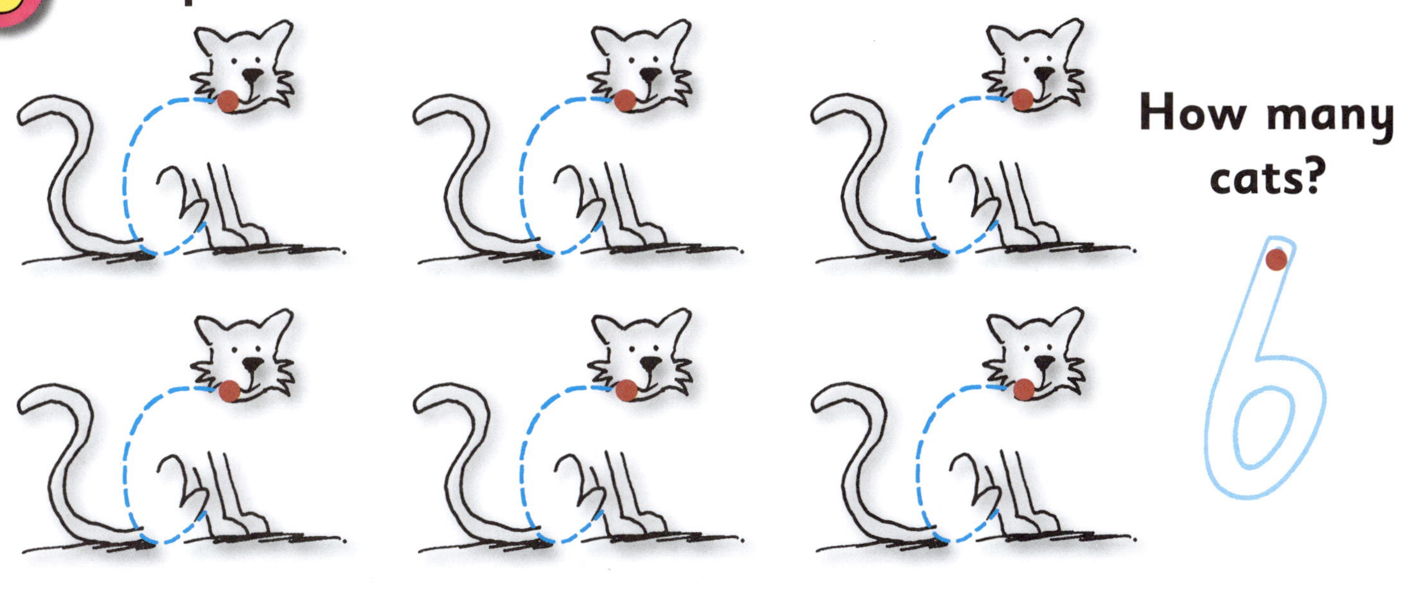

How many cats?

## 4 Track the handles on Charlie's cups.

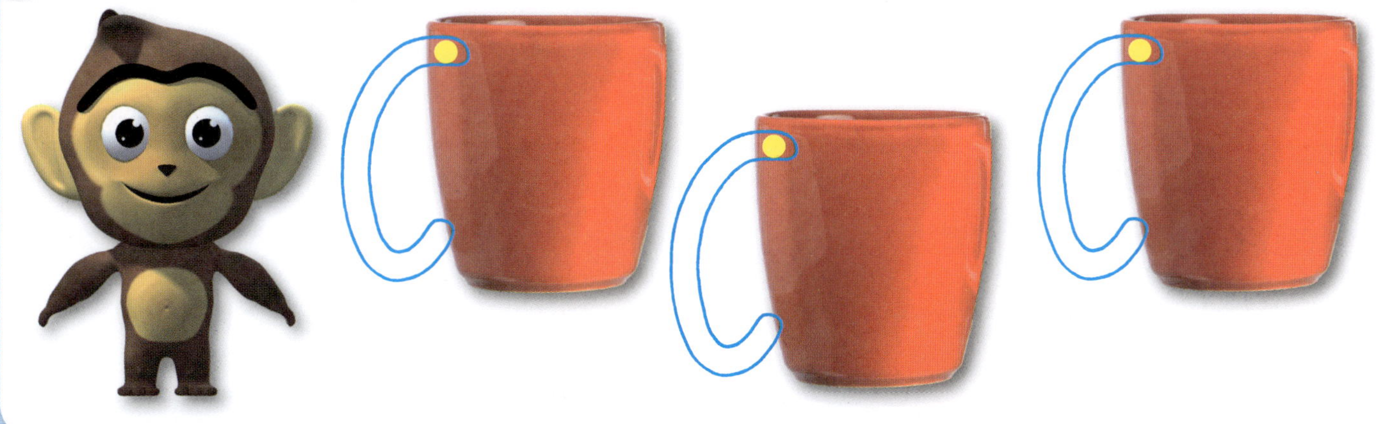

## 5 Trace and write.

# o O

## Lesson 11

Trace.

olive

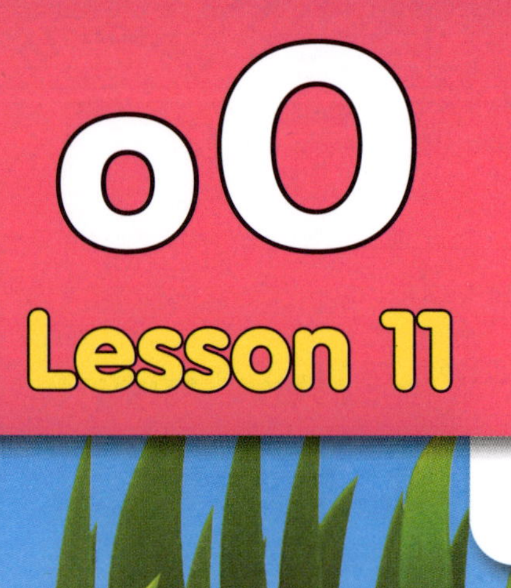

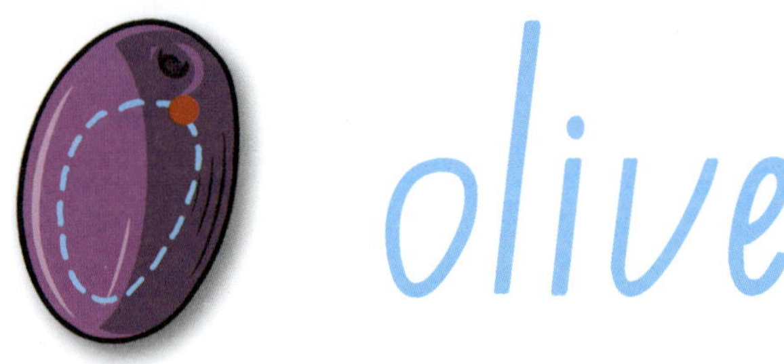

**1** Trace Octo Puss.

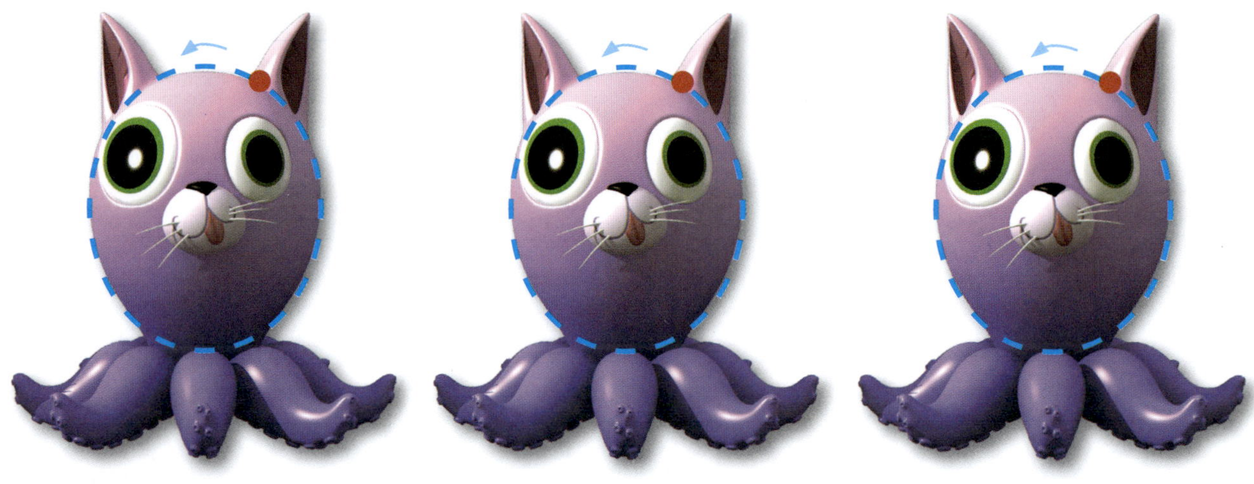

**2** Track the balloons.

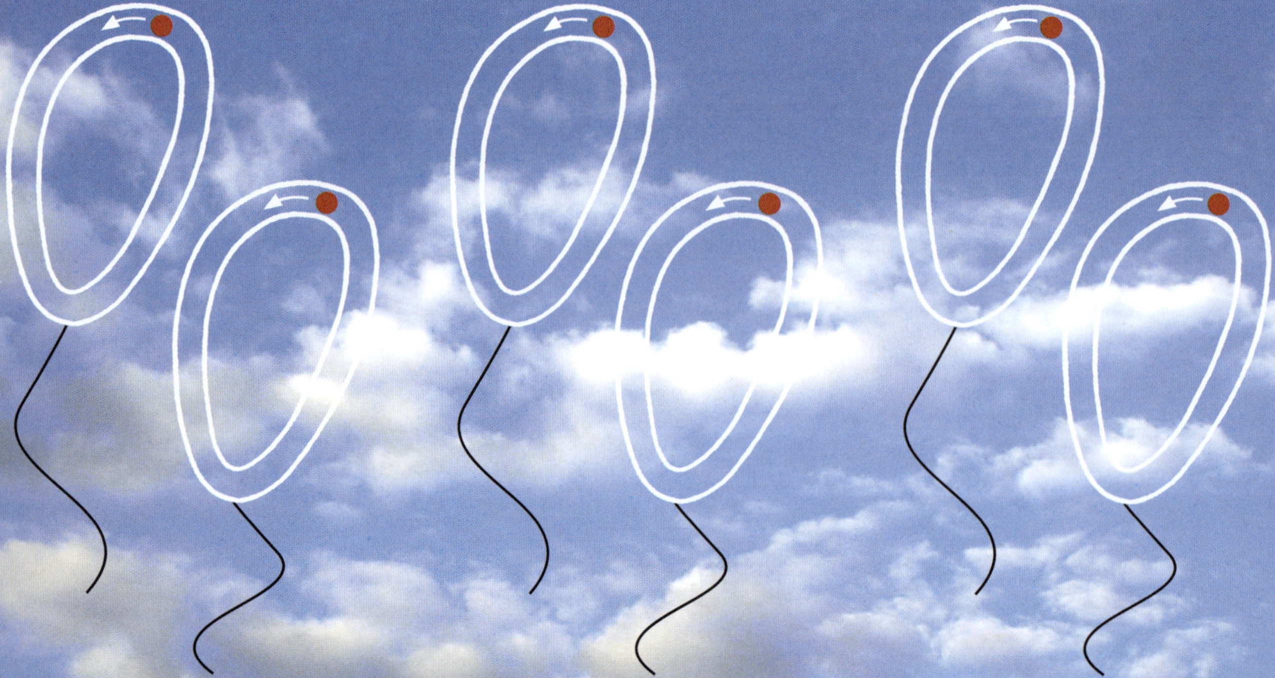

## 3 Trace Queenie Quail's eggs.

## 4 Buzz over to the honey.

## 5 Trace and write.

# uU
## Lesson 12

Trace.

umbrella

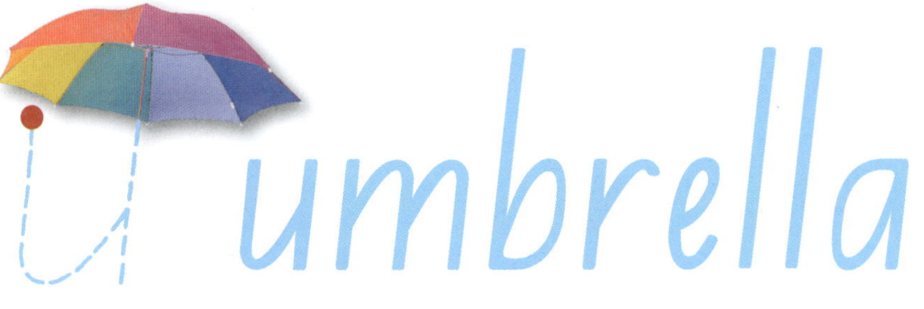

**1** Complete the cup cakes.

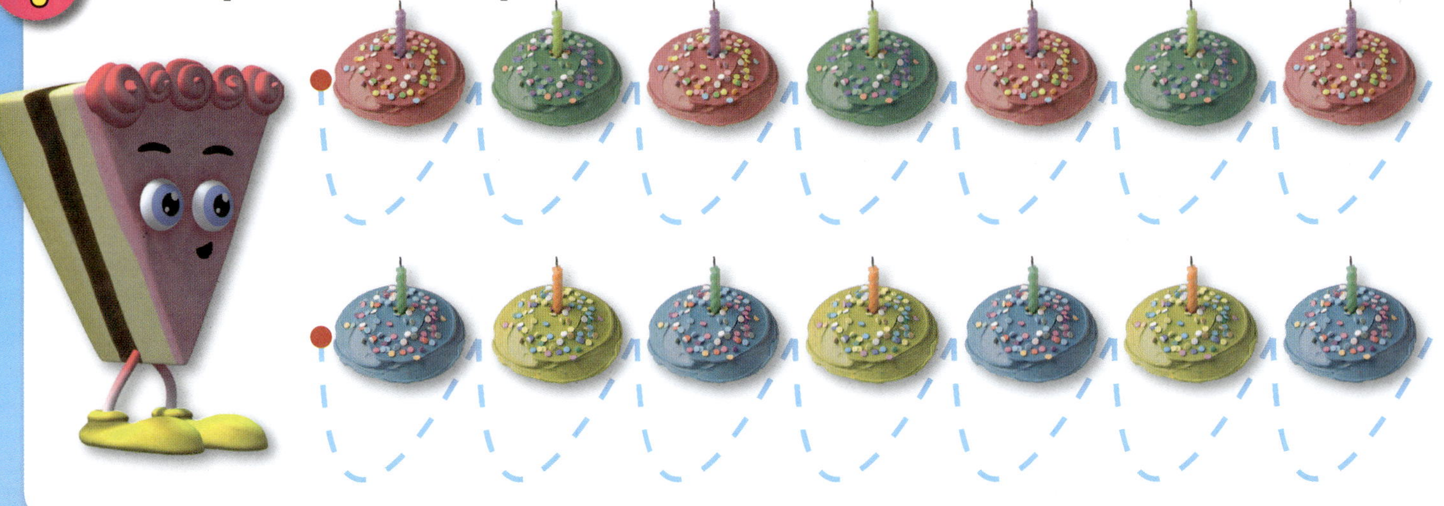

**2** Track the umbrellas.

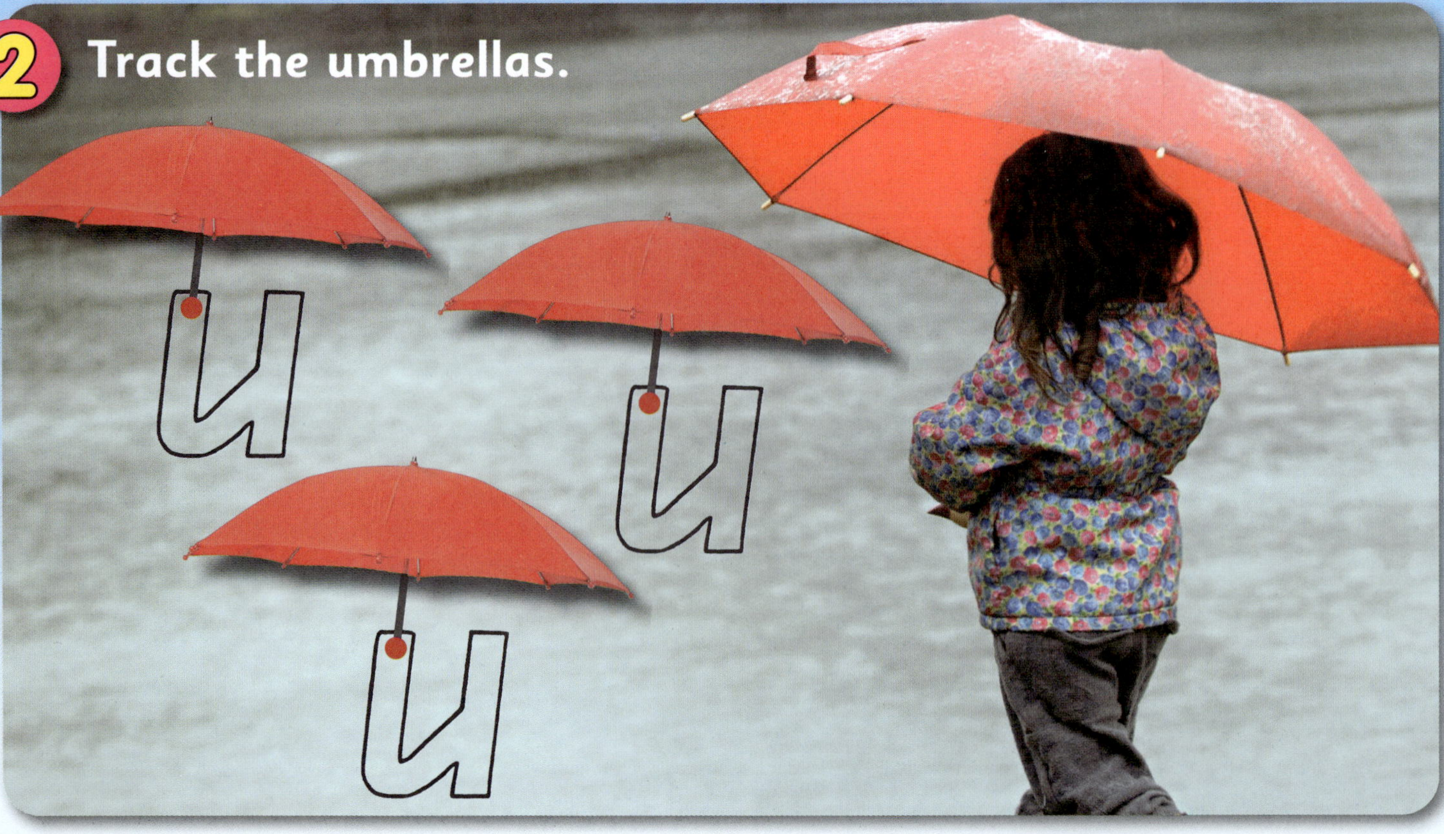

## 3 Draw some friends for Underting.

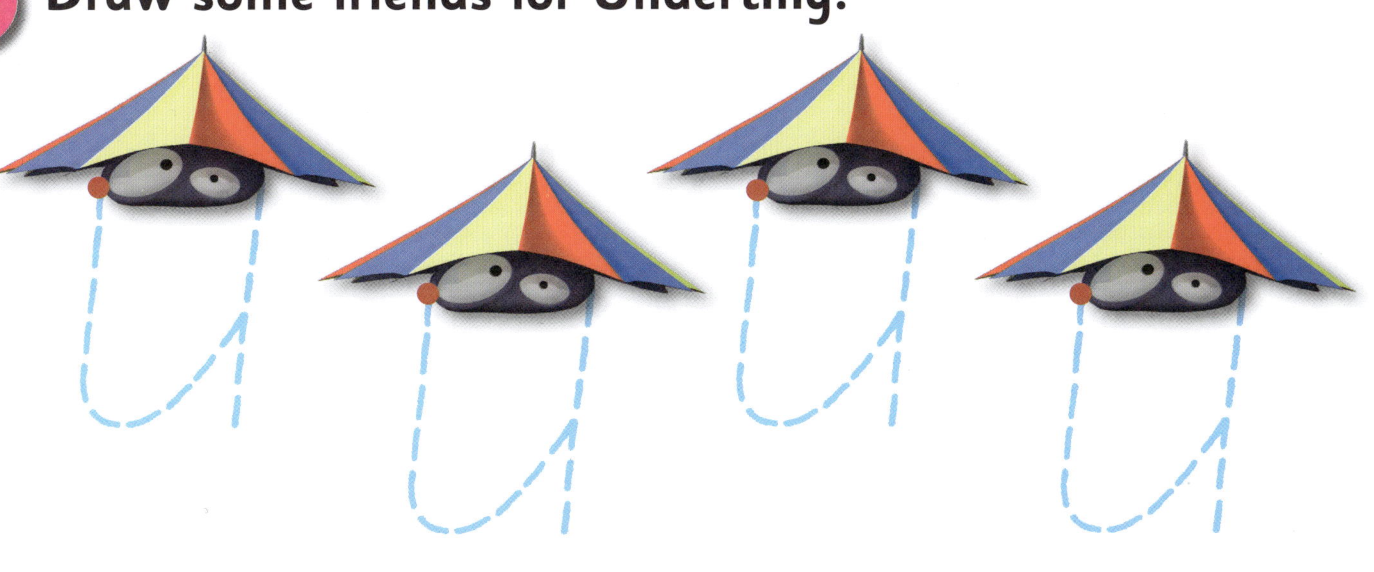

## 4 Complete Red Rabbit's underground holes.

## 5 Trace and write.

u u u u u u u u

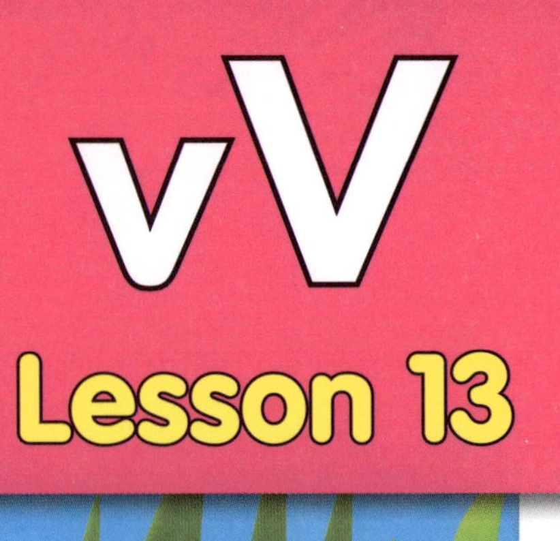


Trace.

vase

1 Draw a vase for each flower.

2 Track each vacuum cleaner.

3 Draw leaves on the trees.

4 Trace each bird's beak.

5 Trace and write.

Trace.

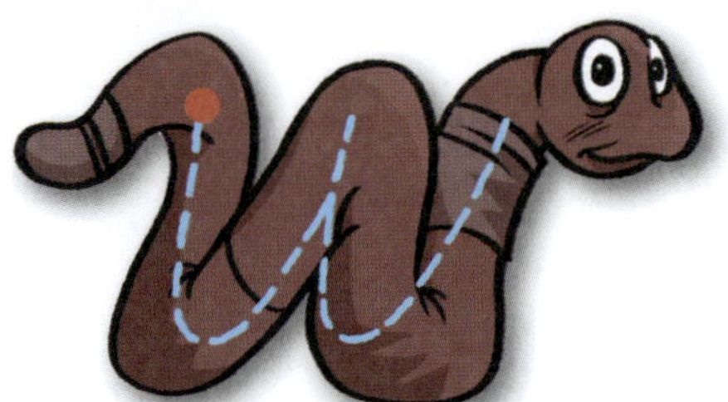

worm

1 Draw waves for Wheely Whale.

2 Finish the turtles' shells.

**3** Help the critters find their things. Track the paths.

**4** Draw the crocodile's teeth.

**5** Trace and write.

# eE
## Lesson 15

Trace.

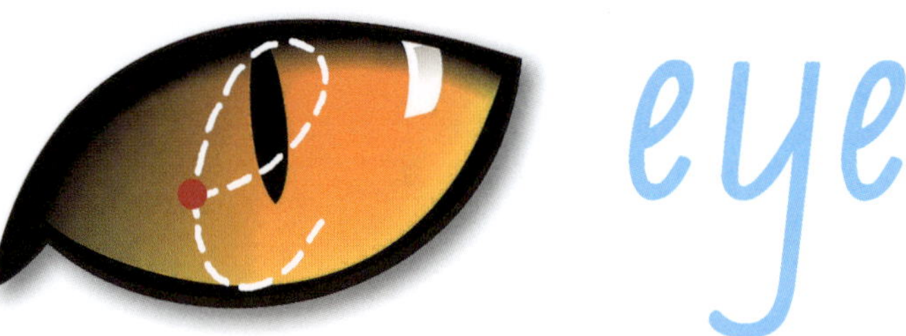


1 Zoom around the track with Eggster.

2 Complete Blue Wing's eggs.

How many eggs?

8

3 Track the patterns on the T-shirts.

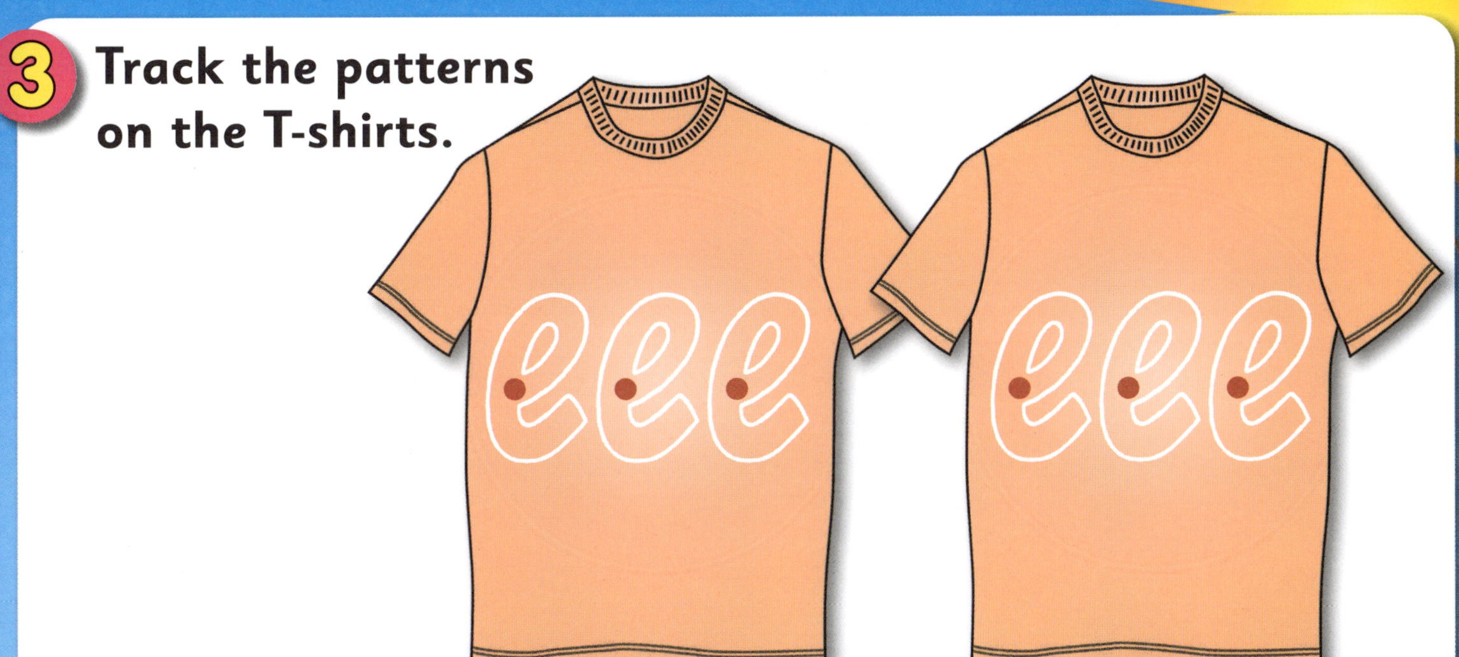

4 Complete the ladders.

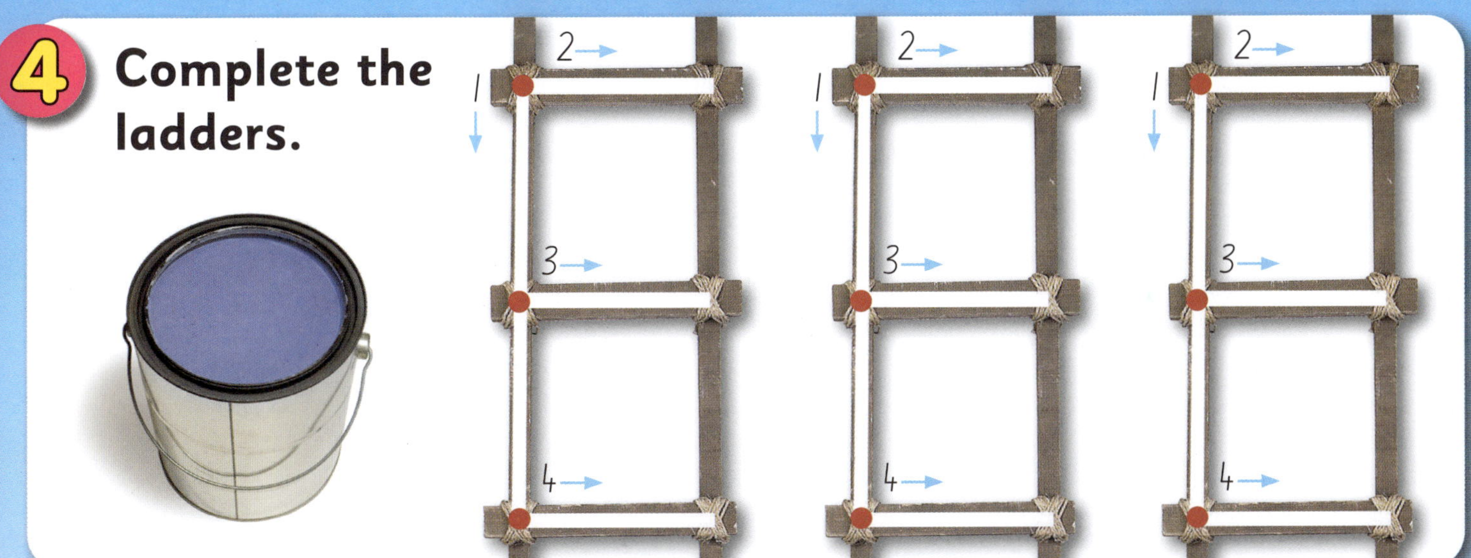


5 Trace and write.

# sS
## Lesson 16

Trace.

snake

**1** Follow Sunny Snail's trails.

**2** Track Jake Snake's friends.

3 Slide down the slippery slides.

4 Trace the steam from Sam's soup.

5 Trace and write.

# Review 2

**Complete each word. Join to the correct picture.**

Octo Puss

whale

snails

apple

Eggster

cake

Alphapet

Underting

water

vase

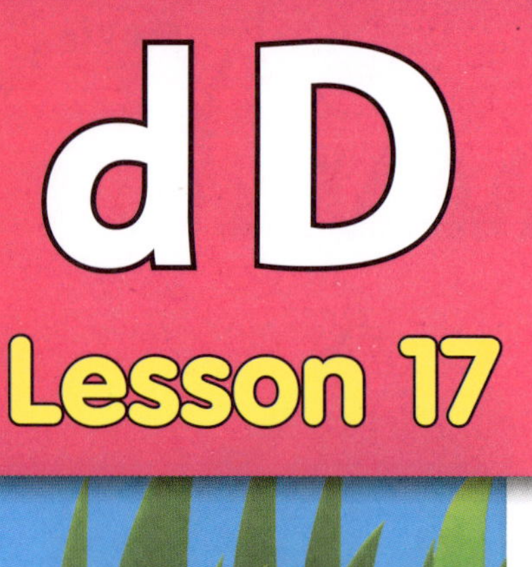

# dD

## Lesson 17

Trace.

dog

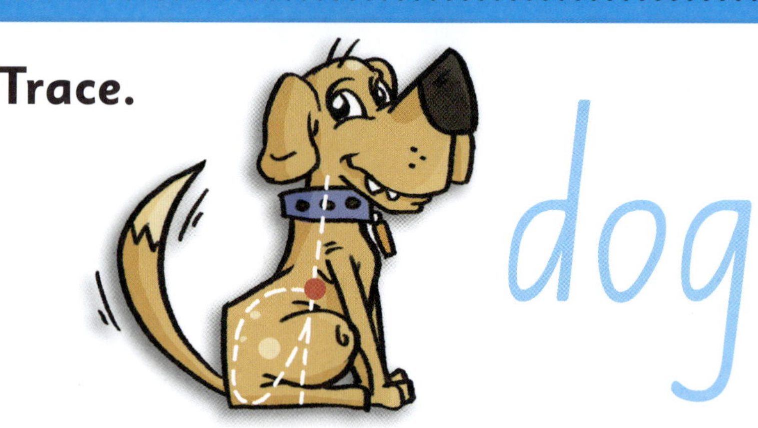

1 Help Dogfin reach his bone. Start at the red dot.

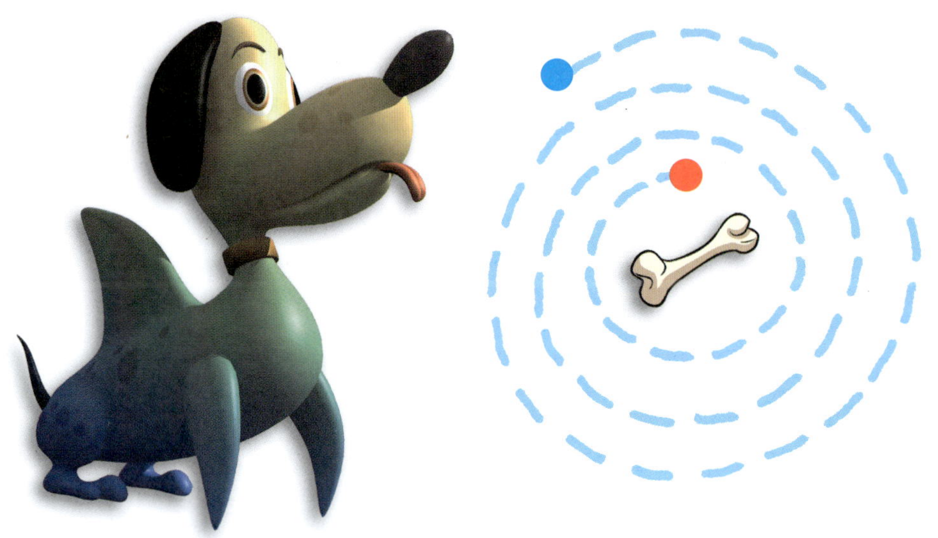

2 Track Dan's soup spoons.

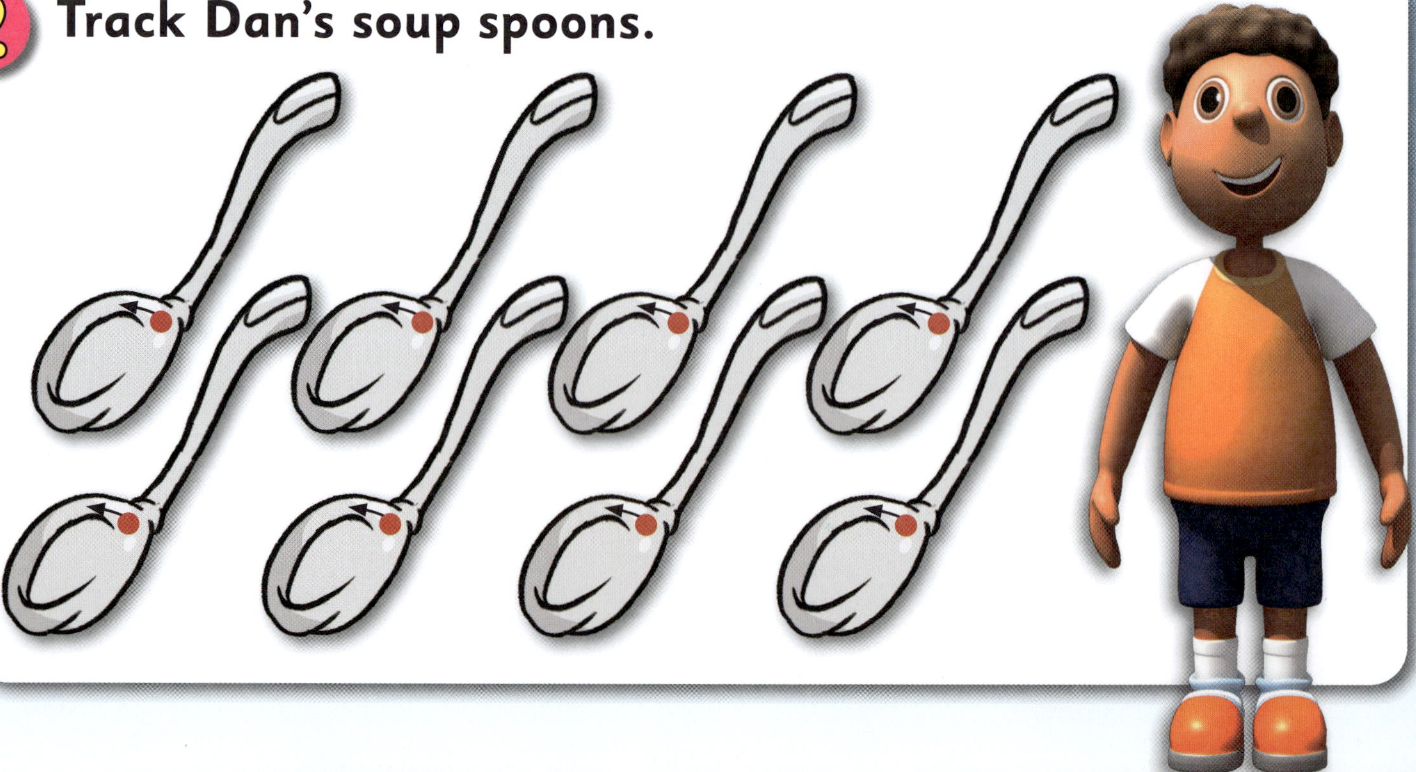

## 3 Trace the dinosaurs.

## 4 Track the handles.



## 5 Trace and write.

# qQ
## Lesson 18

Trace.

**1** Trace the castle roof tiles.

**2** Complete each queen's crown.

3 Trace the dots on Queenie Quail's friends.

4 Complete the balloons.

How many balloons?

10

5 Trace and write.

q q q q q q

1 Trace Yetiyo's yoyos.

2 Trace the pattern.

How many socks?

6

## 3 Complete and colour Baby Face's bibs.

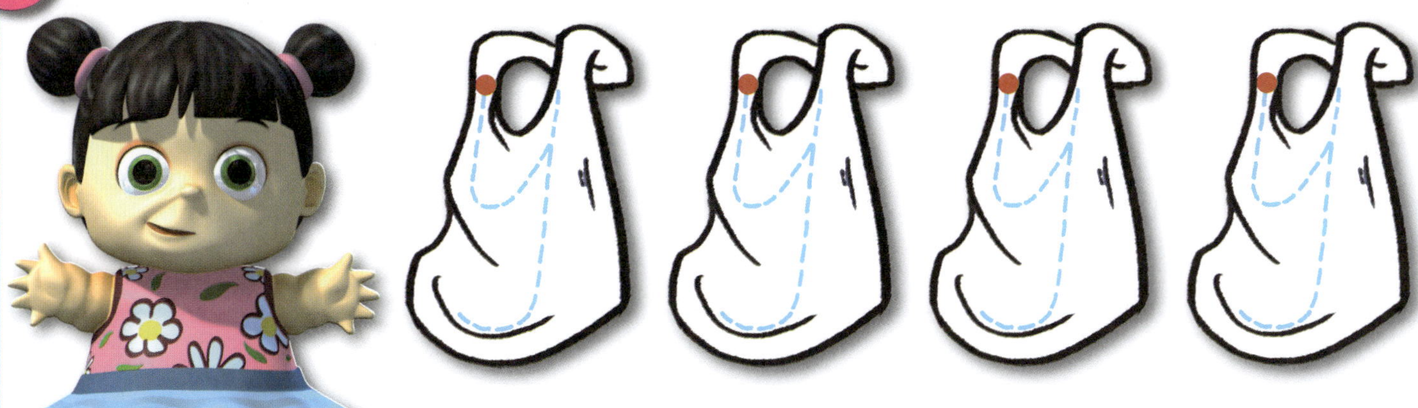

## 4 Trace the sails on the yachts.

## 5 Trace and write.

y y y y y y

1 Trace the wings of Grumble Goz's friends.

2 Track the petals on Issy Me's flowers.

3 Complete Go Go Gizmo's gizmo. Add a few gizmos of your own.

4 Trace the jigsaw pieces.

5 Trace and write.

# Review 3

**Complete each word. Join to the correct picture.**

Grumble Goz

dog

gold

Queenie Quail

yo-yo

quiet
yawn
Dan
ghost
Yetiyo

# nN
## Lesson 21

Trace.

net

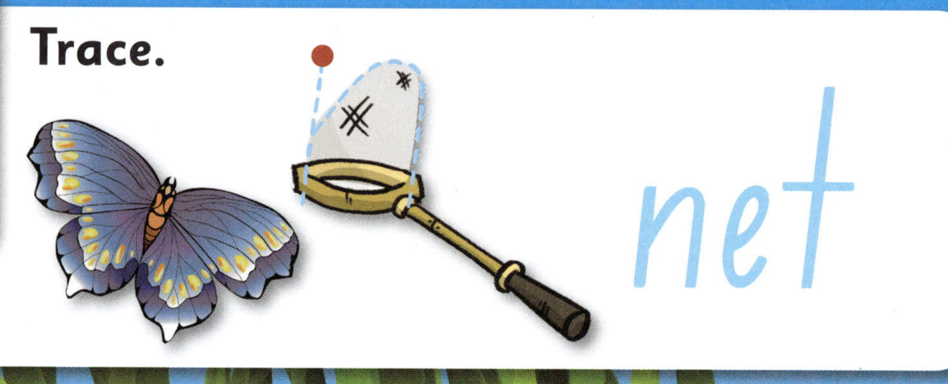

**1** Hop across to Nutty Newt.

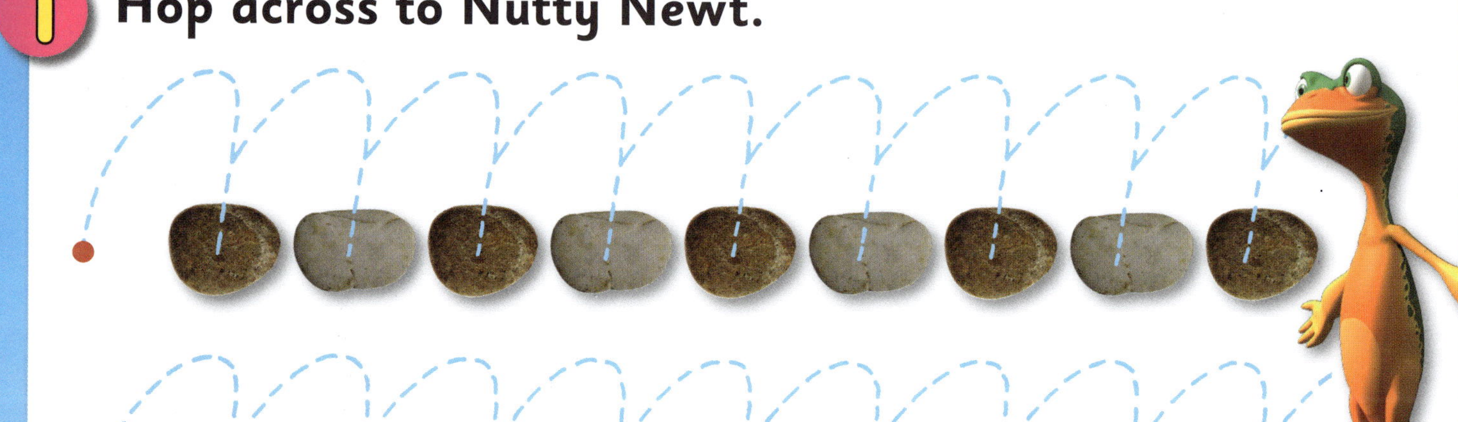

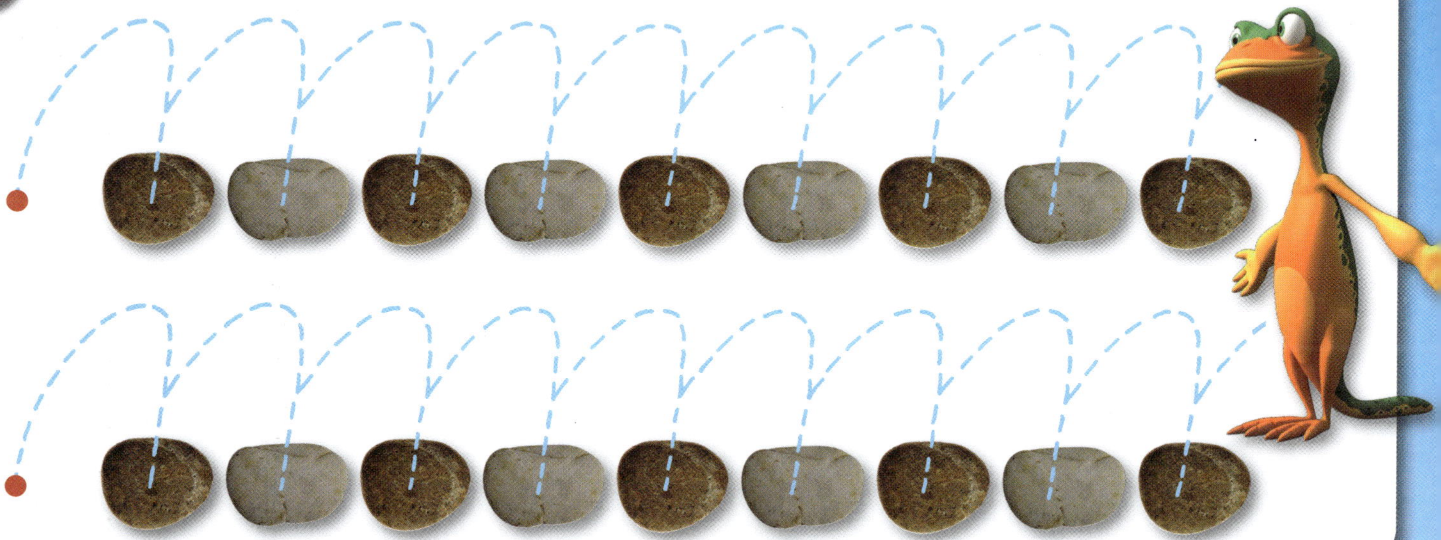

**2** Track Sunny Snail's friends.

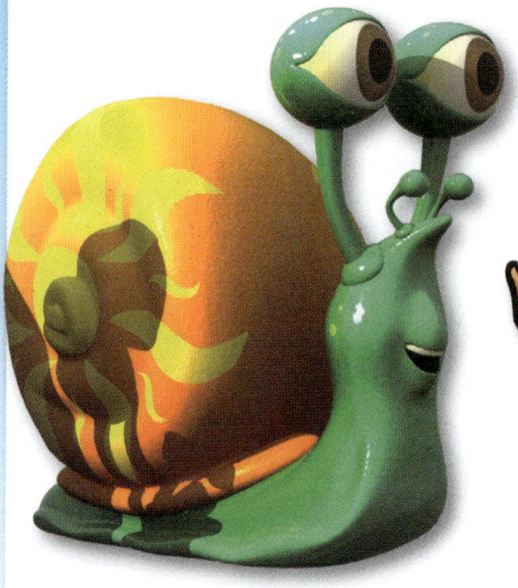

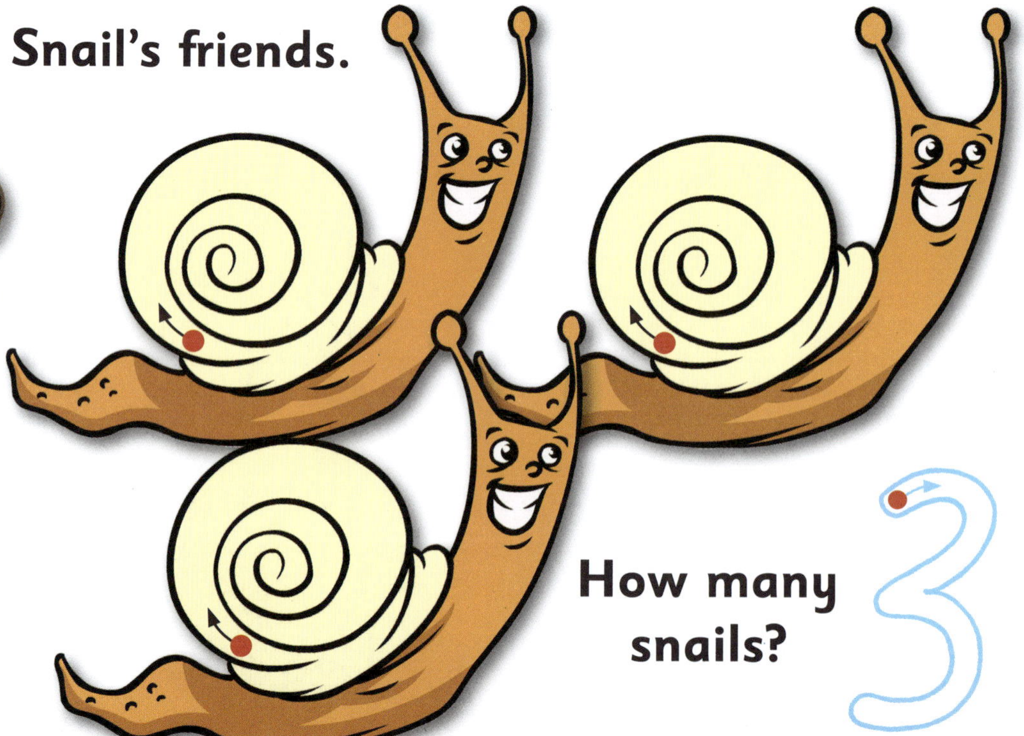

How many snails? 3

## 3 Build new bridges for Gus.

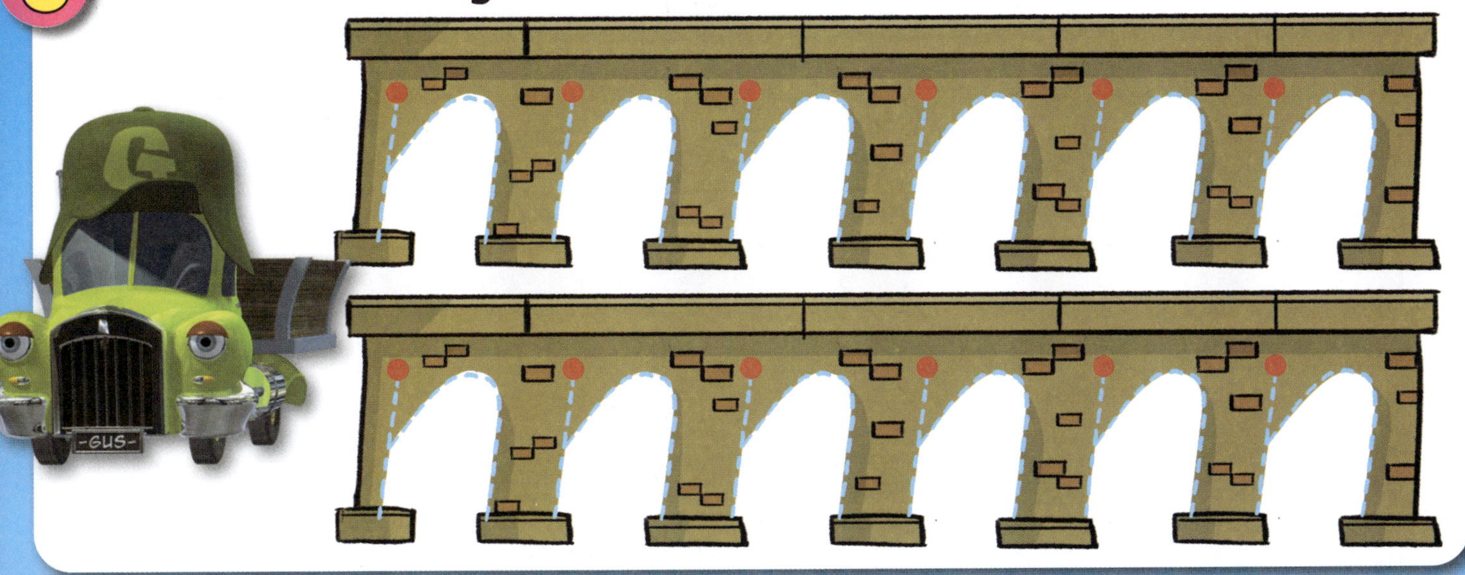


## 4 Trace Horse Hee Hippo's doors.

## 5 Trace and write.

n n n n

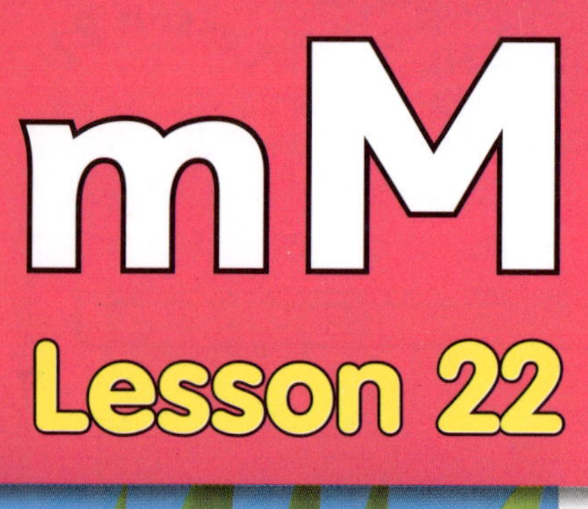

# mM

## Lesson 22

Trace.

mouse

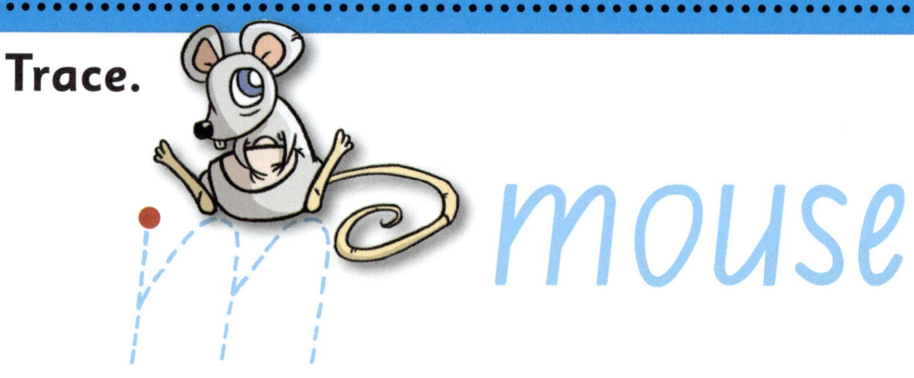

**1** Hop over to the cheese.

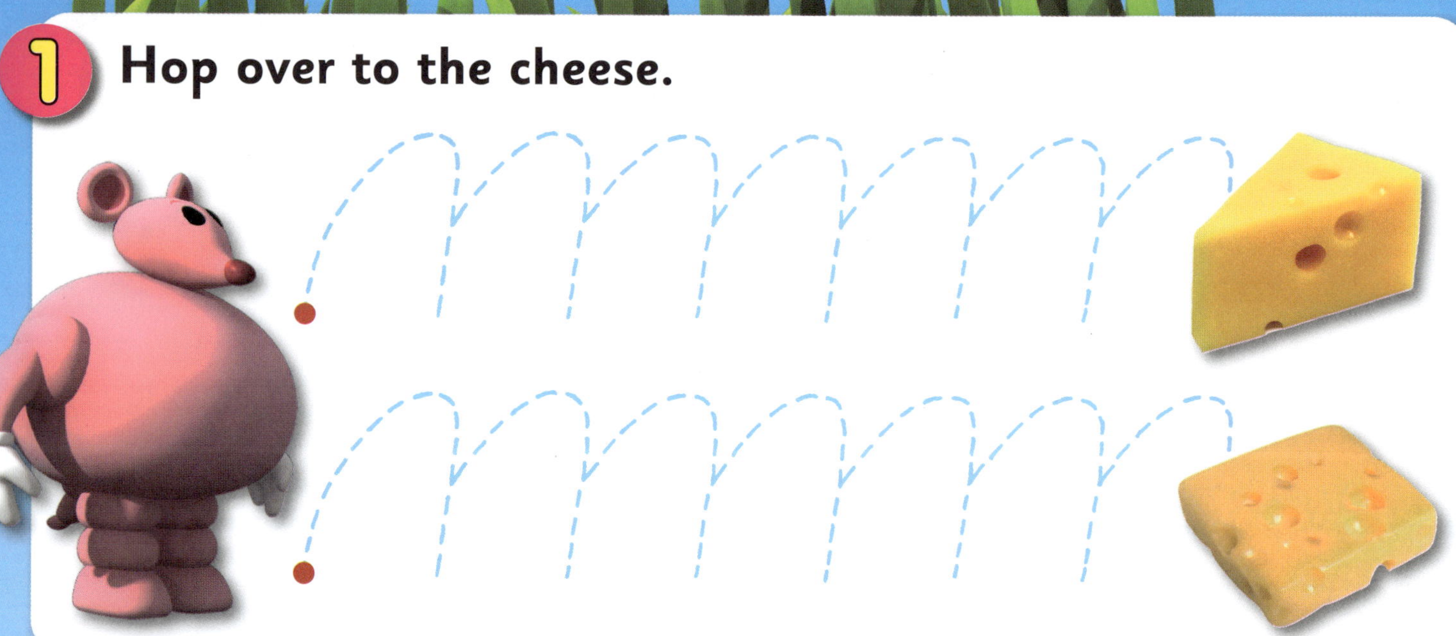

**2** Track. Make some monsters of your own.

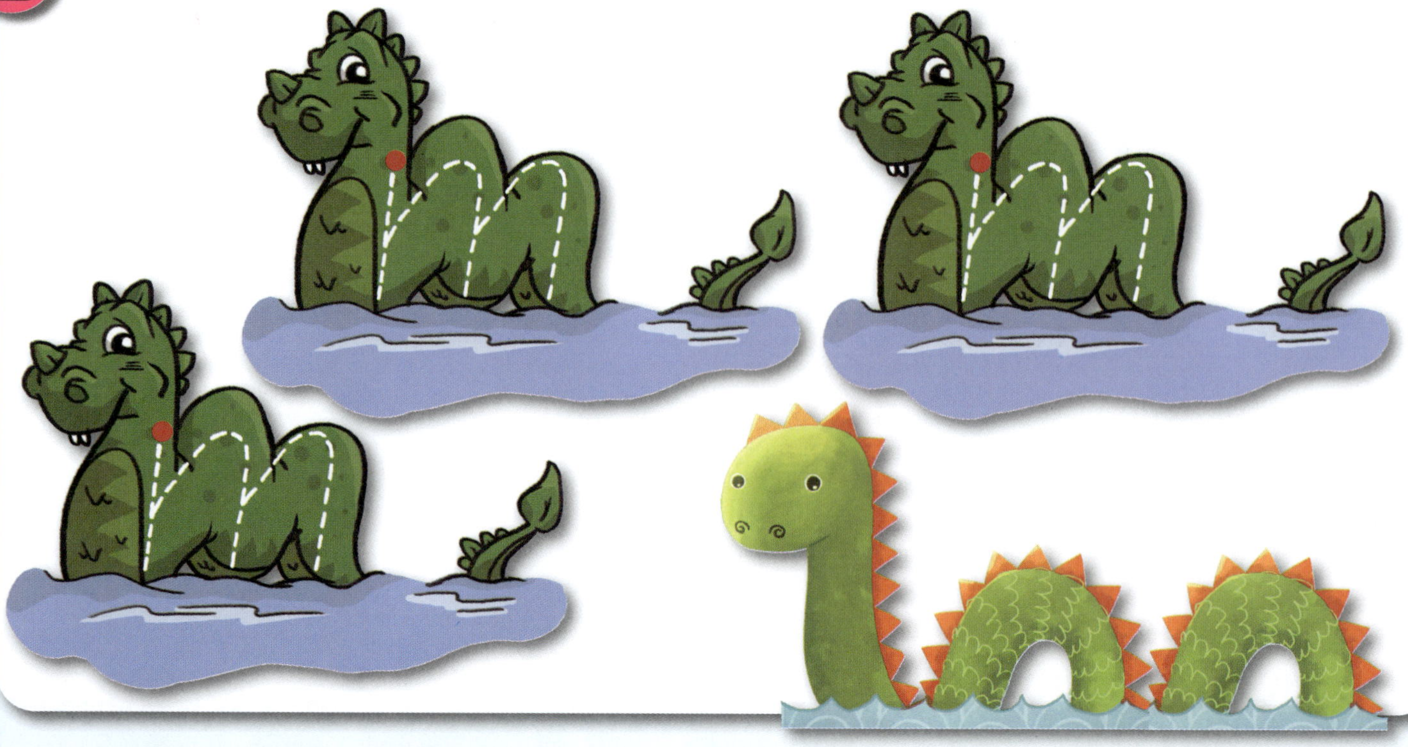

## 3 Decorate the masks.

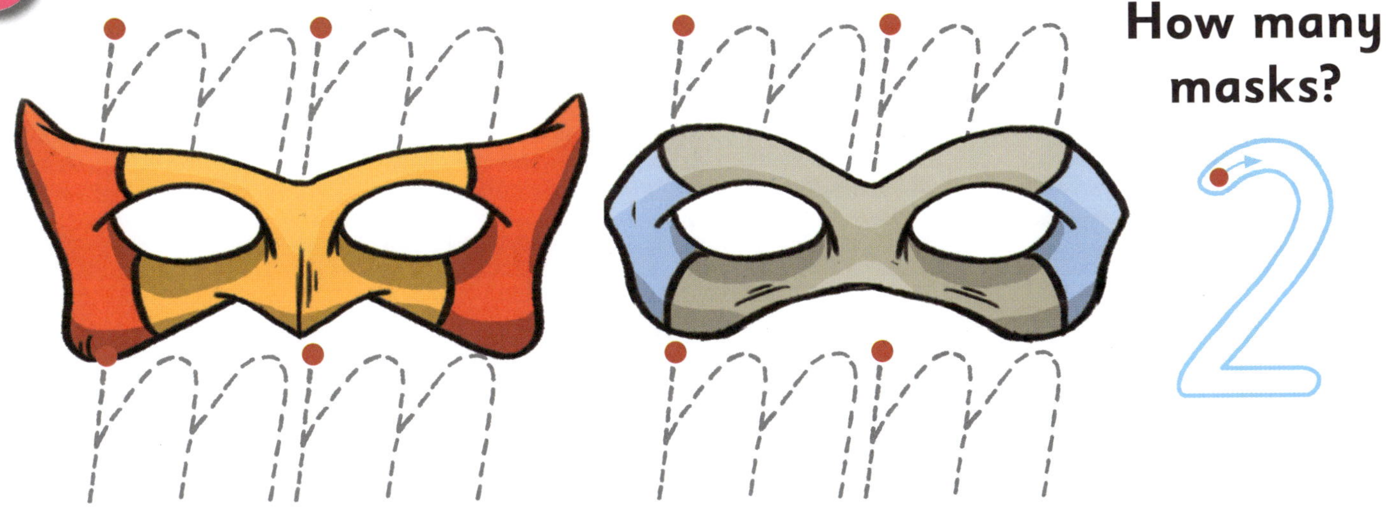

How many masks?

## 4 Complete the royal crowns.

## 5 Trace and write.

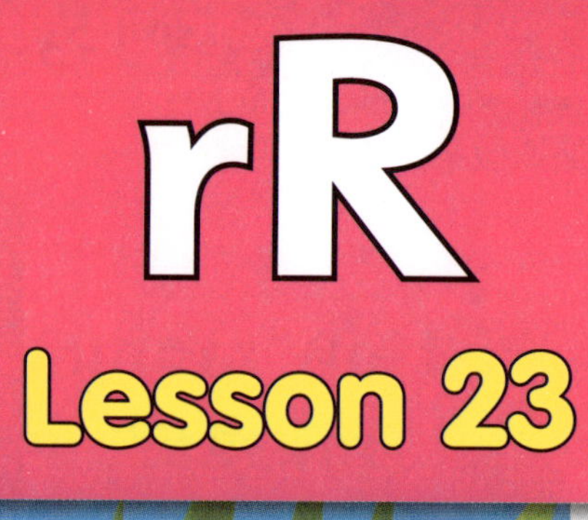

1 Rock around with Rocky Robot.

2 Trace the dots on Red Rooster's roses.

3 Track the taps.

How many taps?

4 Track the robots' arms.

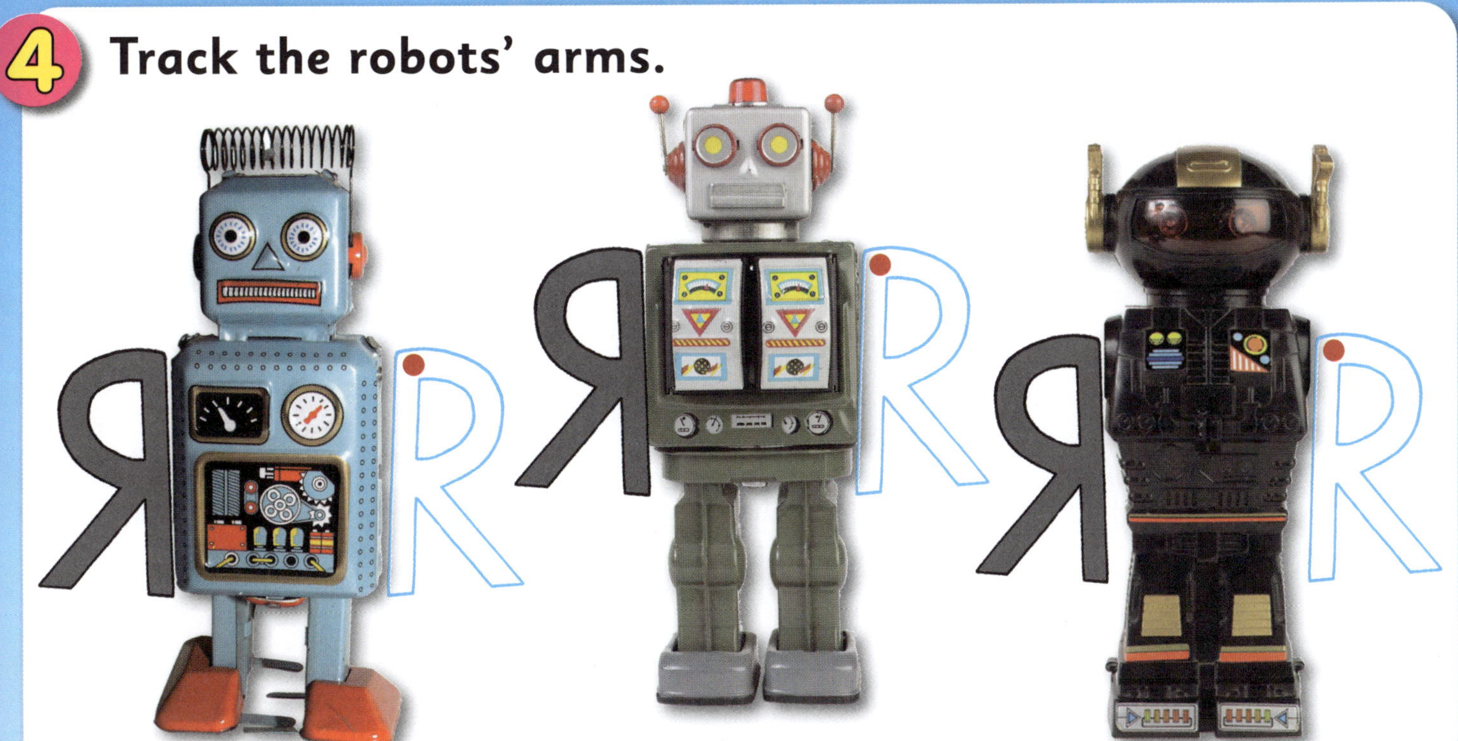

5 Trace and write.

# bB
## Lesson 24

Trace.

**1** Bounce along with Bubble Blow.

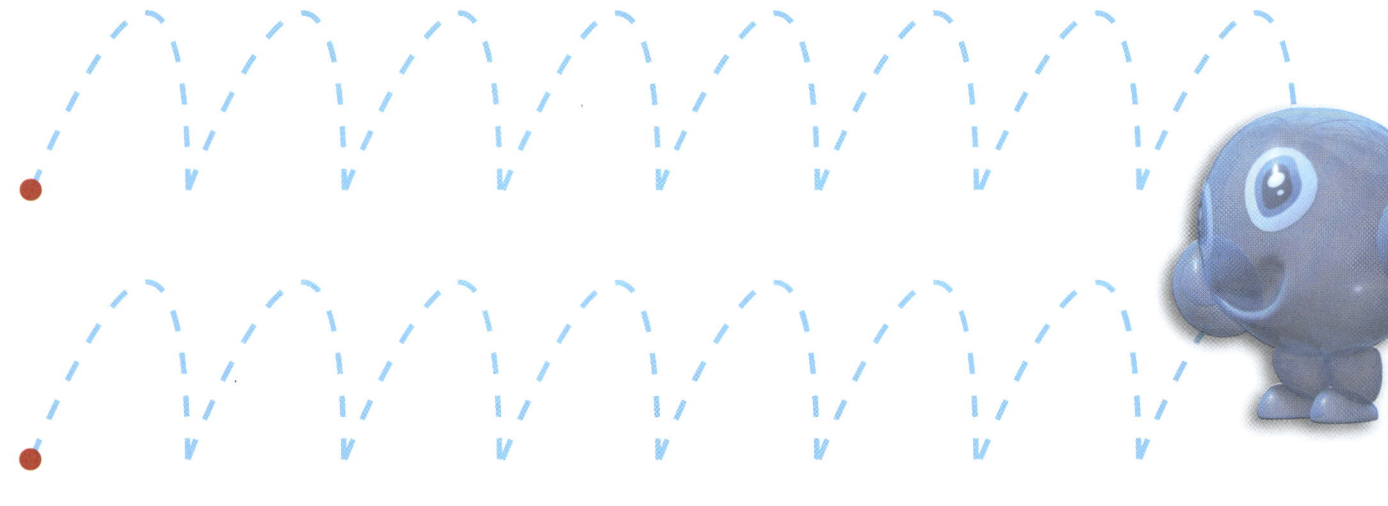

**2** Track Kite Bike's horns.

## 3 Trace the bug's legs.

b b b b b b b b b b

## 4 Complete the beautiful butterflies.

B B B

## 5 Trace and write.

b b b b b b

# hH
## Lesson 25

Trace.

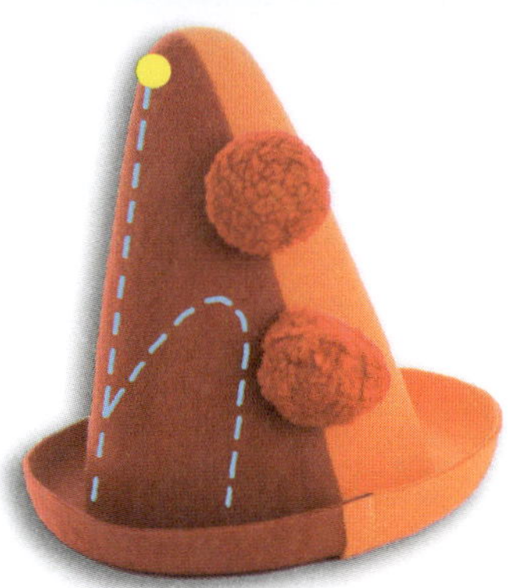

hat

1 Help Happy Nap find her pillow. Start at the red dot.

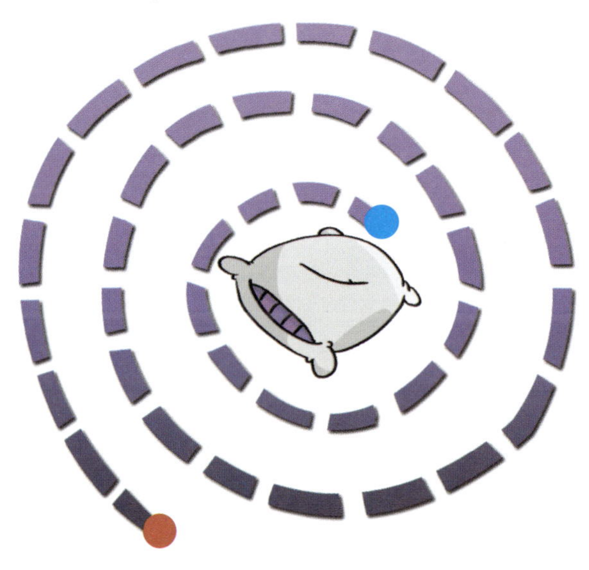

2 Track.

## 3 Trace Horse Hee Hippo's friends.

## 4 Track the chairs.

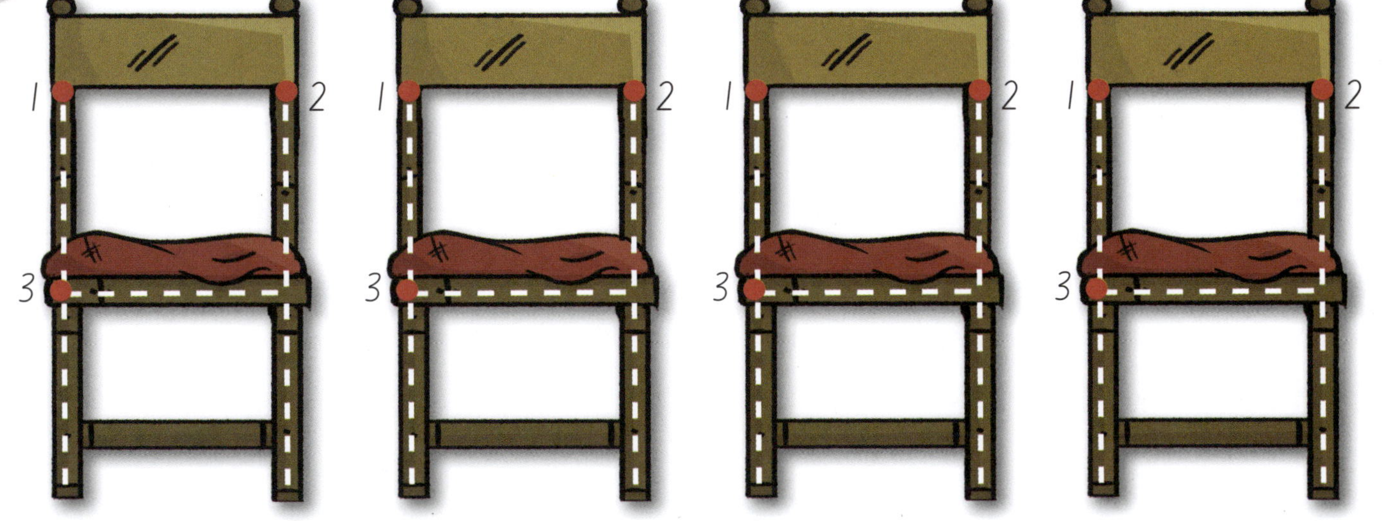


## 5 Trace and write.

h h h

# kK Lesson 26

Trace.

kite

1 Hop about with Kangako.

2 Track the keys.

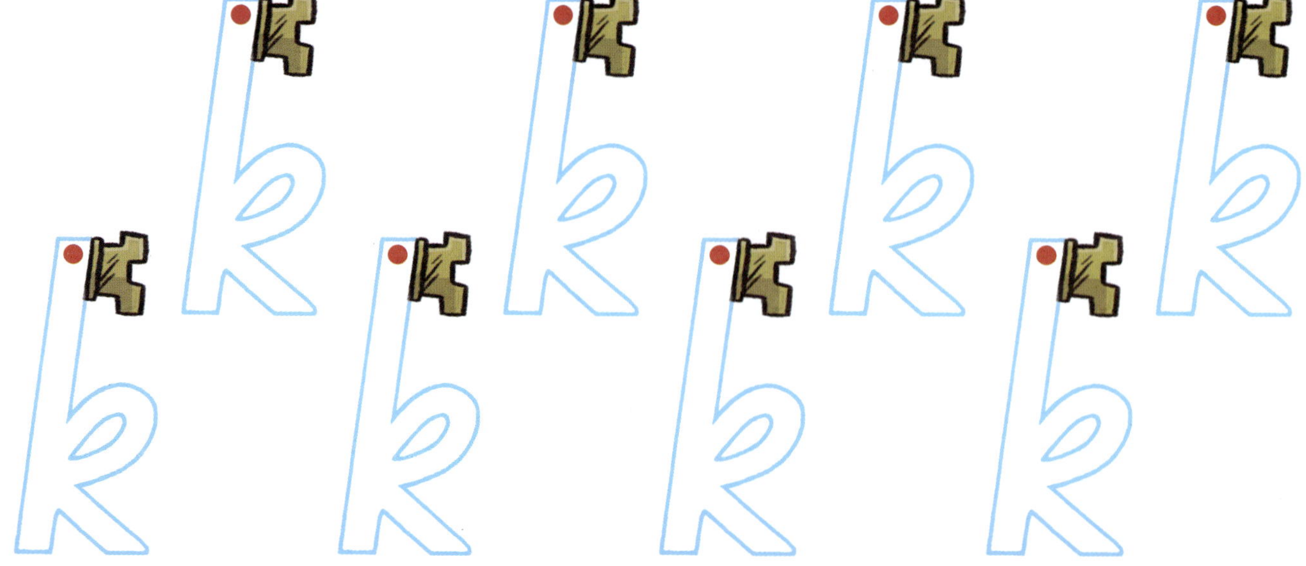

3 Complete Pram Lamb's toy rattles.

4 Track the King's royal shields.

5 Trace and write.

# pP

## Lesson 27

Trace.

pear

1 Catch Penny Drop's coins.

2 Track the handle on each pot.

3 Trace Pinkipoo's friends.

4 Track each pair of scissors.

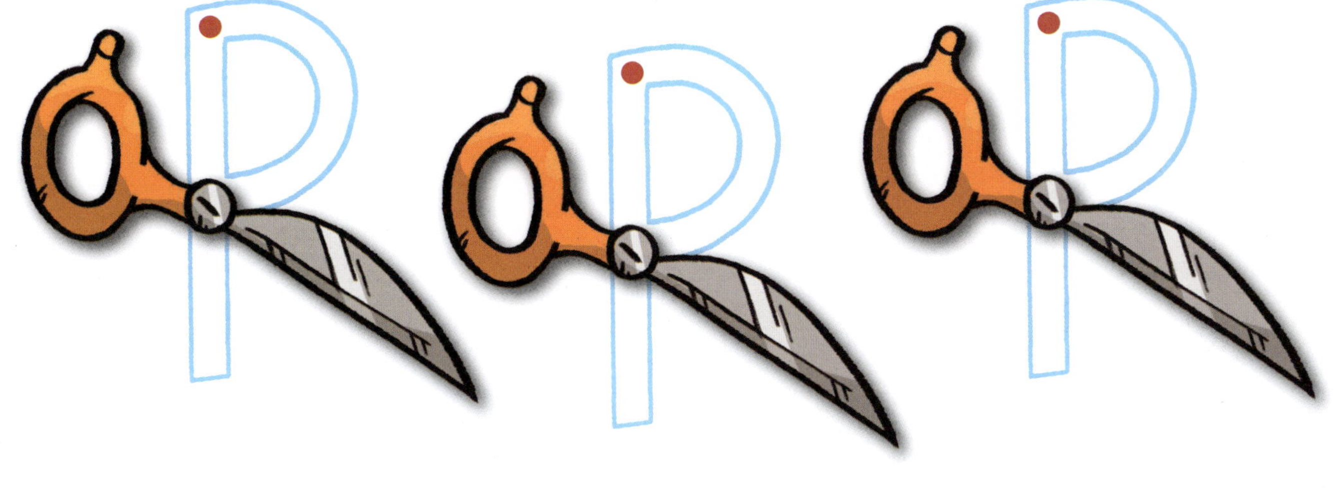

5 Trace and write.

p p p p p p

# Lesson 28 • Number fun

**Join the answers. Write the numbers.**

How many ...

bubbles?

lizards?

eggs?

socks?

legs?

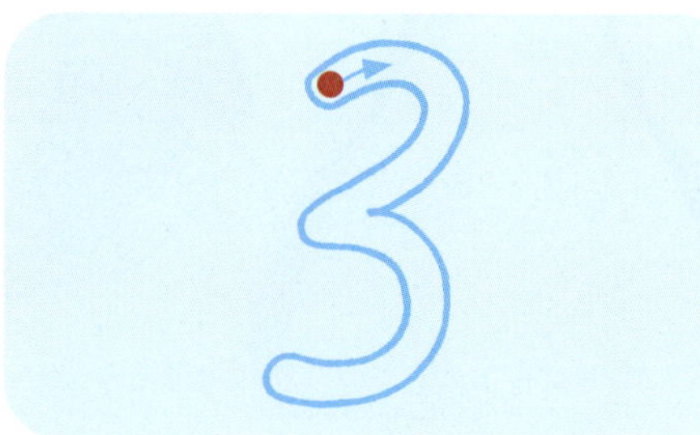


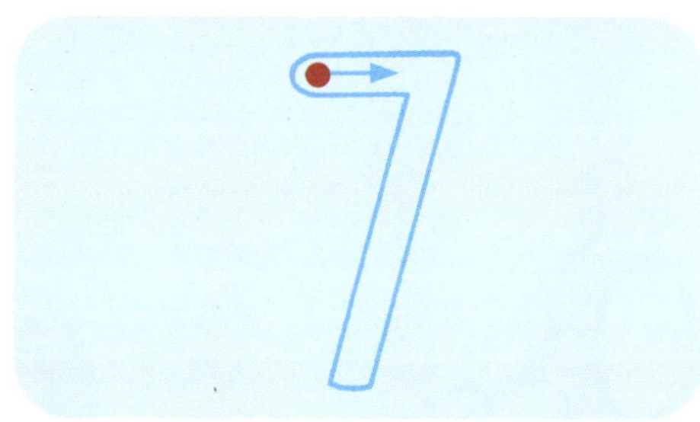


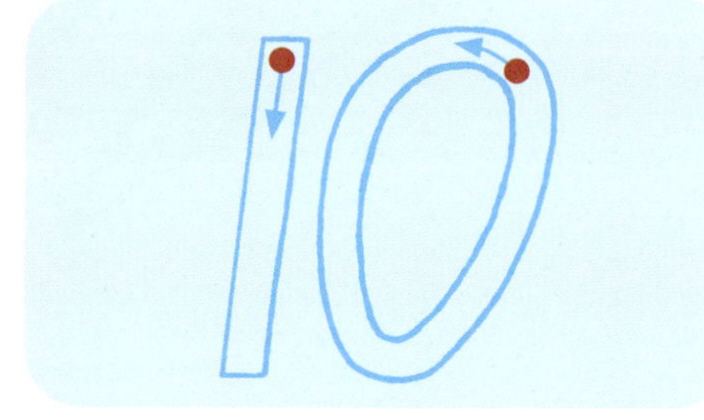


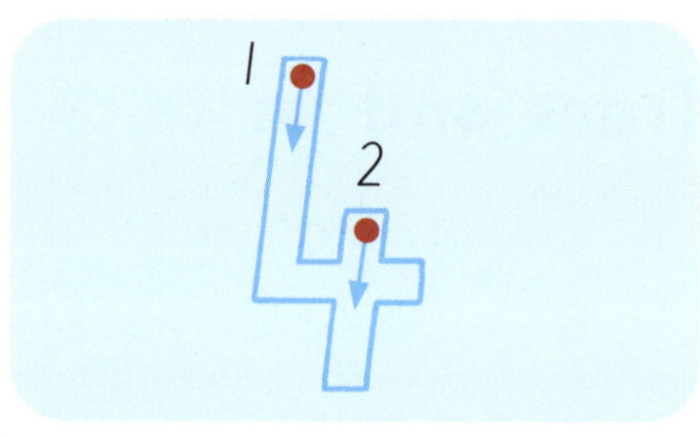

**Join the answers. Write the numbers.**

How many ...

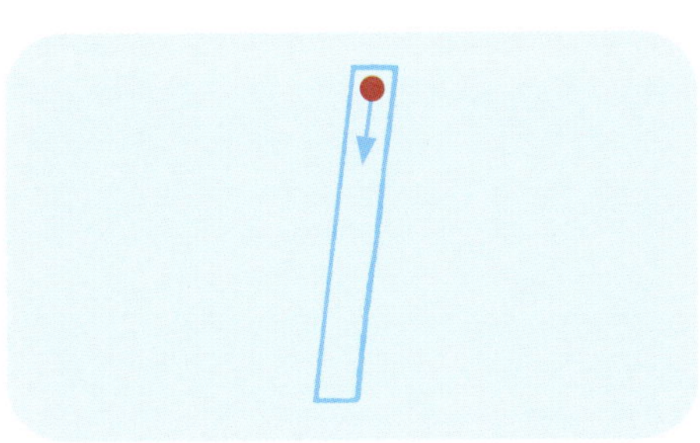


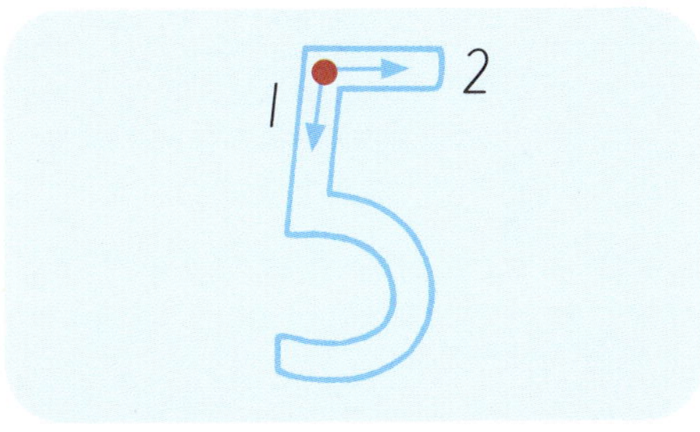


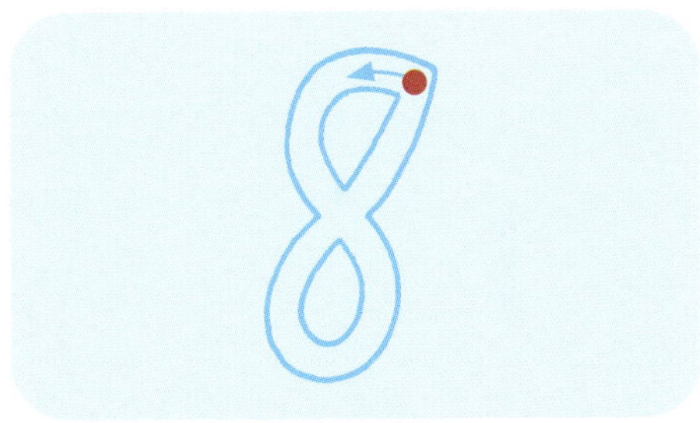


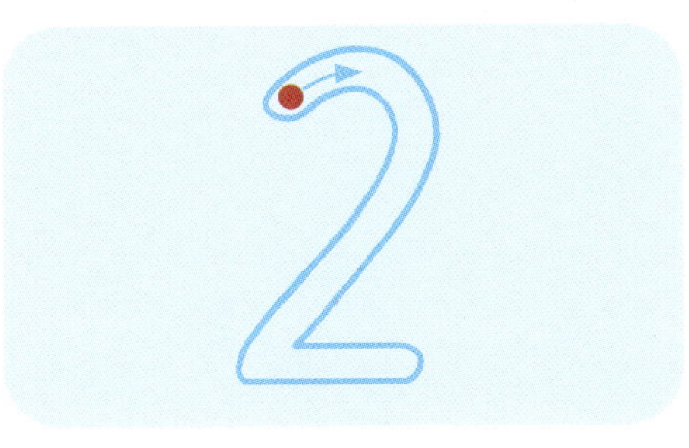


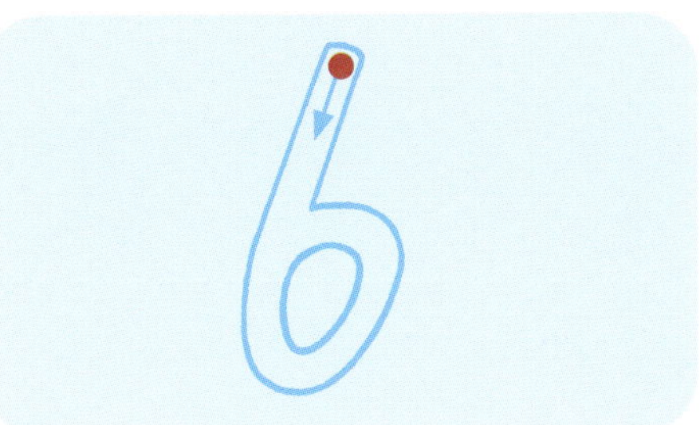

# Fun spot 2

## 1 Trace and colour.

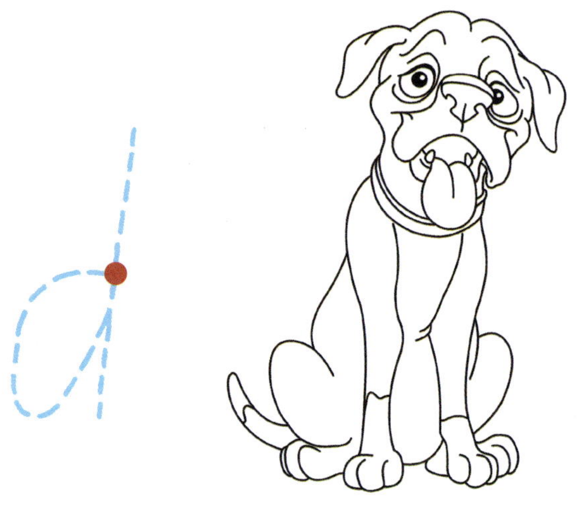

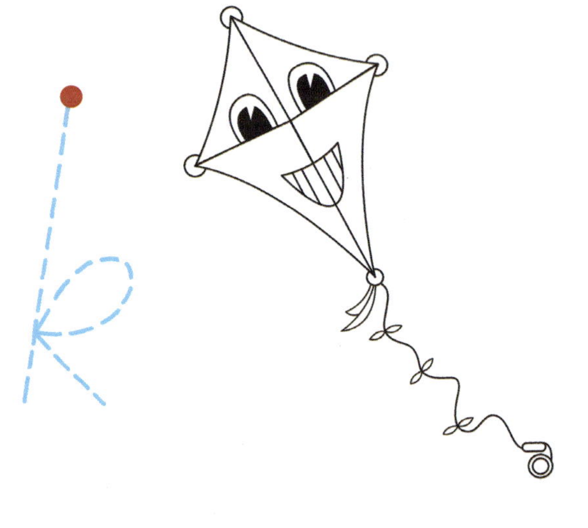

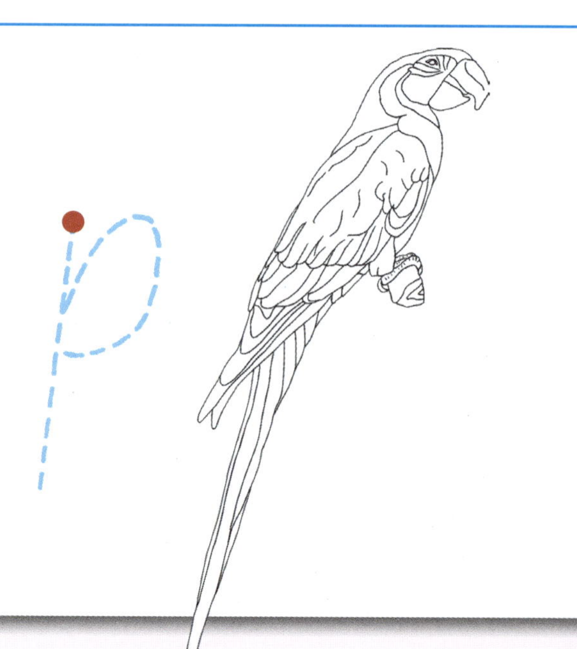

## 2 Write the beginning letter of each critter's name.

______ ______ ______ ______

## 3 Trace Kangako's bounces.

# Review 4

**Complete each word. Join to the correct picture.**

Red Rabbit

hat

mouse

Blue Wing

robot

key
Nutty Newt
bubbles
Happy Nap
paper

# Practice 1

Trace.

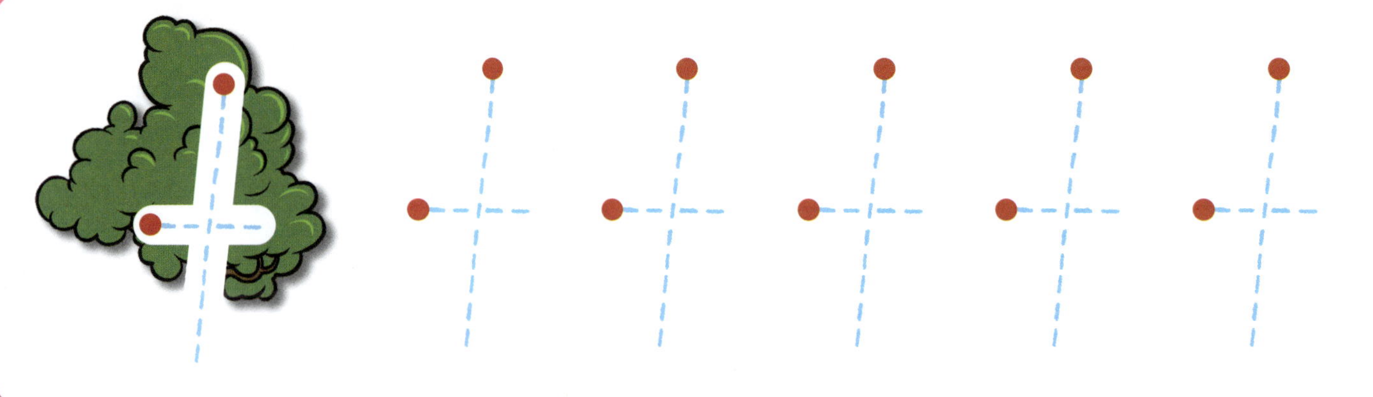

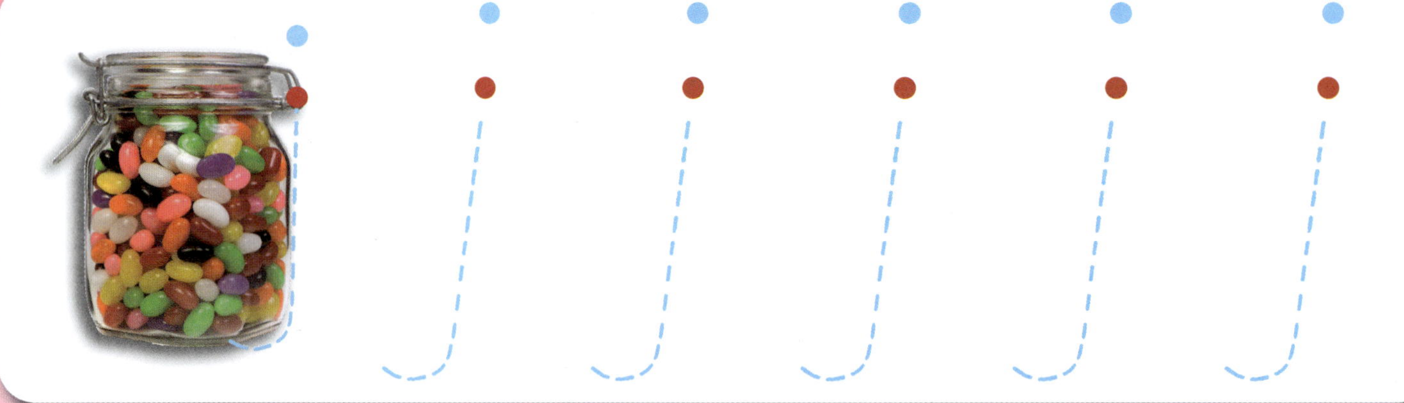

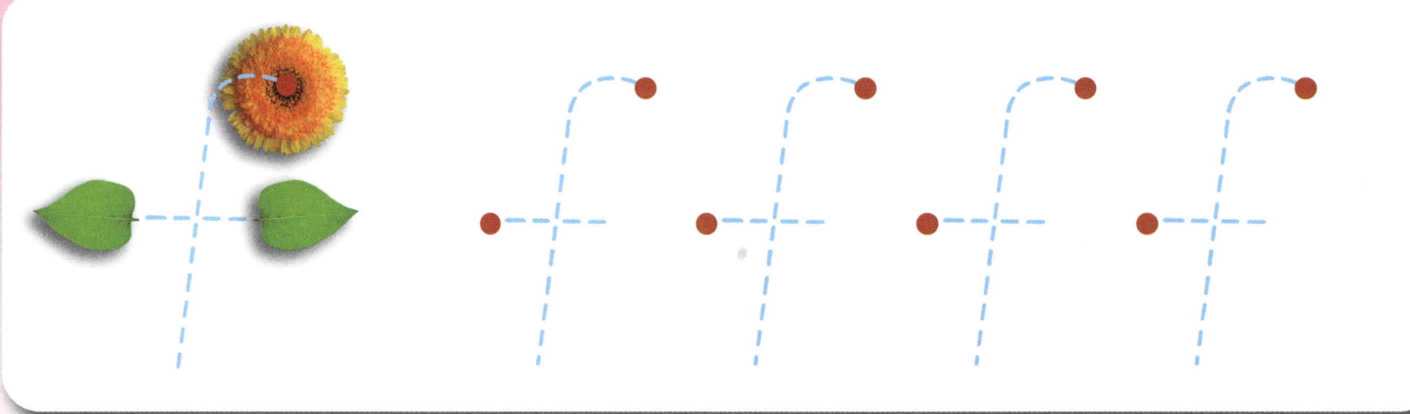

**Trace.**

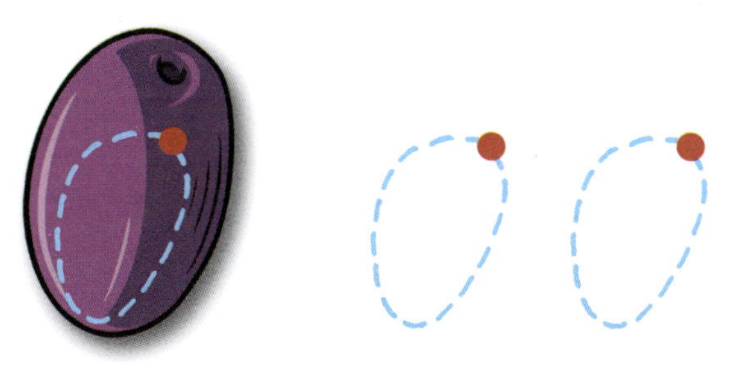

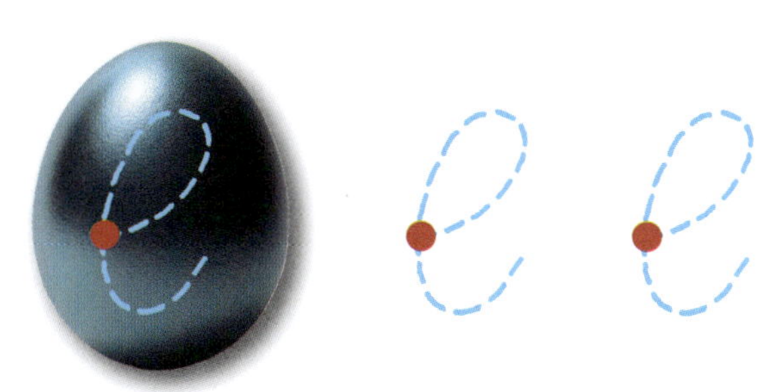

# Practice 2

Trace.

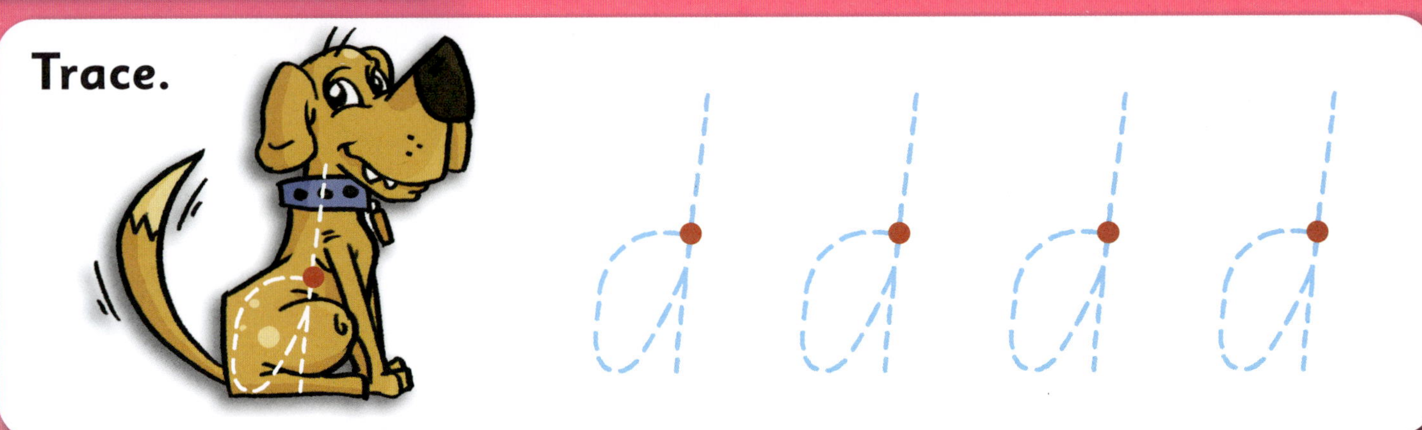

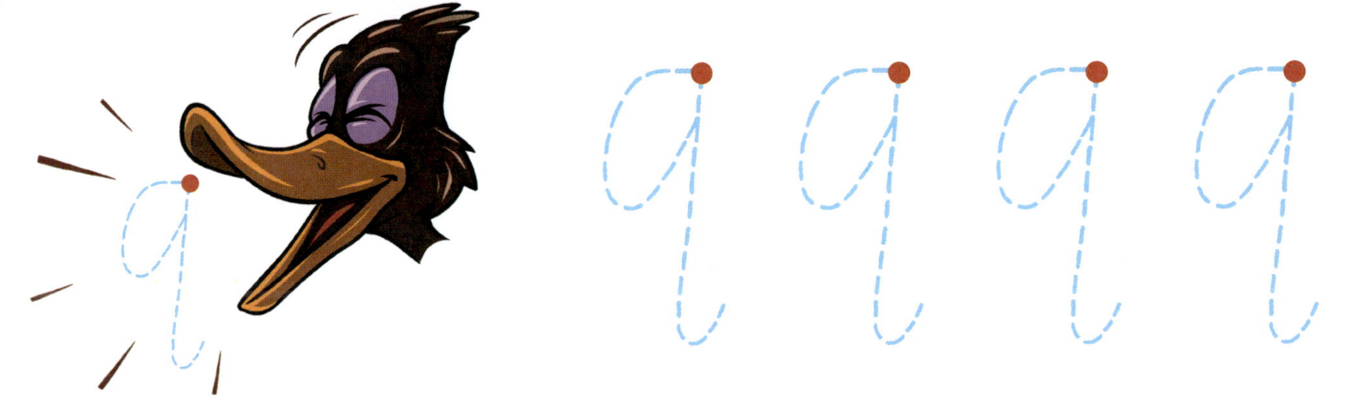

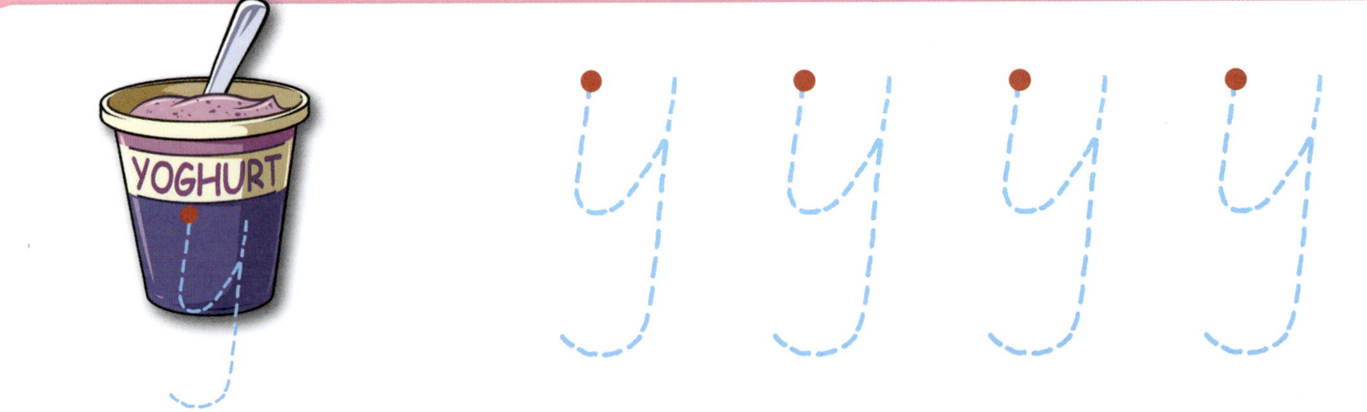

Trace.

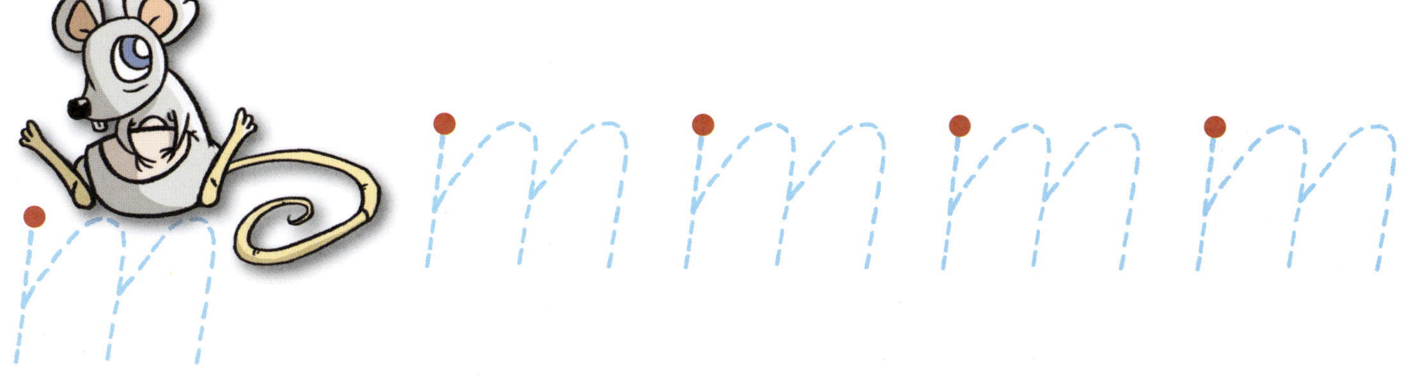

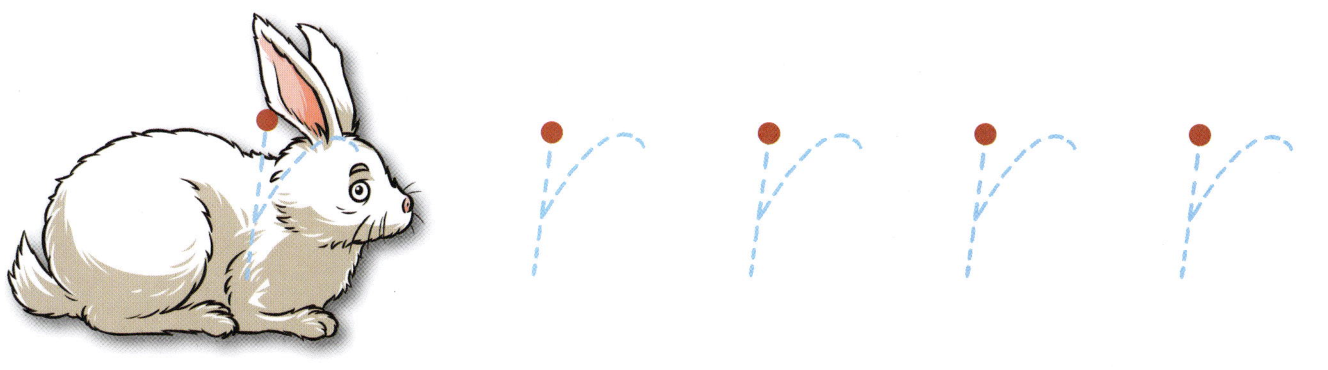

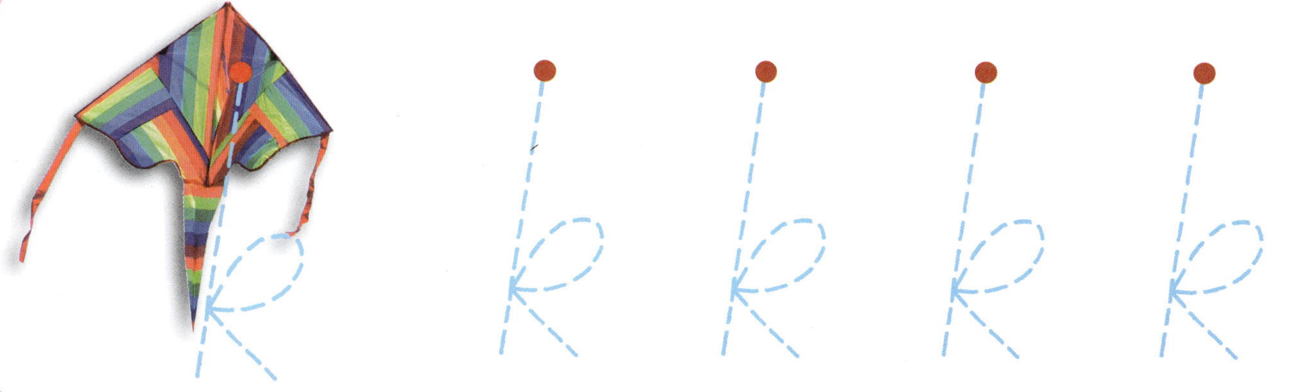

ABC
Reading
eggs
Excellent
handwriting!